Even the gr
will End
will alw

S111~ 2£1

Audry Sibindi
& Grace Maworera

Tales of

Nursing in
Diaspora

20 Candid Stories of
Nurses' Experiences in Diaspora

Copyright © Audry Sibindi and Grace Maworera

Published by: Tales in Diaspora Publishing

First publication: 2020

Audry Sibindi and Grace Maworera have asserted their right to be identified as the authors of this work in accordance with the Copyright, Designs and Patents Act 1988.

A CIP catalogue record for this title is available from the British Library

ISBN 978-1-9164378-2-1

Book Design by Loulita Gill Design

Printed and bound by IngramSpark, www.ingramspark.com

www.talesindiaspora.com

Acknowledgements

This second book in the diaspora series has been made possible thanks to the following people and organisations:

- The twenty anonymous contributors, who have shared their experiences of nursing in diaspora and donated their share of profits to a charity that supports healthcare improvement in developing countries.
- Alison Carson, who edited all the stories to ensure they are communicated in the best possible way for our readers.
- Loulita Gill at Loulita Gill Design, who designed our cover and internal layout.
- The National Lottery Community Fund, whose grant helped to fund this publication.
- Tales in Diaspora Publishing, who published this book.
- The unsung heroes who have supported us in this venture.

Thank you all very much!

More
Tales in Diaspora

This book is the second in a series of six about life in diaspora.

The first book in this series Tales of Living in Diaspora contains 16 candid short stories of life in diaspora and is available to purchase online and in all major bookstores.

Our future publications have the following working titles:

Tales of Success/Succeeding in Diaspora
Tales of Marriages/Relationships in Diaspora
Tales of Raising Children/Parenting in Diaspora
Tales of Working in Diaspora

Are you currently living in diaspora? Would you like to share your experiences in one of these upcoming books? If so, please email us at tales@talesindiaspora.com and indicate the publication for which your story is suitable.

All contributors will be remunerated and credited, but please note that most stories will be published anonymously. However, if you would like to contribute to the book about succeeding in diaspora and you would like people to be able to contact you for more information, then please include all relevant contact details in your tale.

Contents

Introduction

This second book in the diaspora series is dedicated to the valuable and essential profession of nursing. It contains twenty short stories that reveal what it's really like to work as a nurse in another country, also known as diaspora.

For decades, migrant workers have been an accepted part of international healthcare systems, though this is most evident in high-income countries. In the UK, for example, the National Health Service (NHS) has actively recruited overseas doctors and nurses since the 1930s. A 2019 report published by the Nuffield Trust showed the true extent to which the NHS now depends on its foreign workers, highlighting that 23% of its hospital staff were born outside of the UK[1].

It was quite by coincidence that the stories contained in these pages were written, compiled and edited just before and during the global COVID-19 pandemic. While healthcare professionals worked tirelessly and selflessly to treat patients with an unknown

---

1   https://www.nuffieldtrust.org.uk/news-item/one-in-four-hospital-staff-born-outside-the-uk-new-nuffield-trust-analysis-reveals

infectious disease, the world seemed to suddenly wake-up to the true worth of these individuals – of every nationality – and they were appreciated like never before.

While the story of each contributing nurse is unique, one cannot fail to notice that racism is a theme that runs throughout, especially for those from a BAME (Black, Asian and Minority Ethnic) background. The reoccurrence of this issue was not intentional, but it serves to emphasise one of the significant challenges faced by BAME frontline workers in first-world countries. These are the same BAME nurses whose actions, along with those of their Caucasian colleagues, were celebrated at the height of the aforementioned pandemic.

We hope that this book will have many and far-reaching benefits, including:

That it will play a part in disclosing the inequalities, challenges and successes in healthcare services that nurses in diaspora have experienced.

That these accounts will go some way to seeing inequalities eliminated entirely.

That these stories will help readers to further appreciate frontline workers as professionals in their field, especially the immigrants who have made endless sacrifices and endured untold discrimination to care for others.

That these first-hand experiential testimonies will serve as a guide to those considering nursing.

That newly qualified nurses who are looking for a job can gain insight into the career options that are available to them.

That it can be used as a guide to help any nurse who is thinking of migrating to diaspora to continue their career; that they will be aware of the potential challenges and setbacks, the pros and cons, and the endless opportunities of career development.

* * *

Please note that all contributors are anonymous; to protect their identities, all identifiable features have been removed, and pseudonyms are used in place of real names. All content reflects the opinions of the individual contributors.

As a nurse, we have the opportunity to
heal the heart, mind, soul and body of
our patients, their families and ourselves.
They may forget your name, but they will
never forget how you made them feel.

MAYA ANGELOU

1

The Immigrant Nurse

B ed capacity was always challenged when there was no consultant at the weekend to review, discharge or actively treat their patients. That said, with an influx of patients through A&E, staff moved Anne to a surgical ward with the expectation that she would be discharged the next day and thus make space for a colorectal patient that would be in admission long-term. That following day being a Monday, the corridors were buzzing with consultants and their teams pacing around, interested in finding out how their patients had fared over the weekend.

Unexpectedly, the call came that I was needed on the surgical ward. A patient would not let anyone else take out the rest of their surgical wound clips. The patient specifically asked for an immigrant student nurse with only two years' experience to handle it.

Greeted with a warm welcome on arrival, Anne was relieved that I had been called and had come in. Meticulously working through the staples, I could see how the story would unfold long afterwards – my colleagues, who felt very easy to tease and make fun of me, would continue to do so for a long time to come. It was just friendly banter, though. And what did it matter considering a staple-free wound, a happy patient, and a pack of whiskey samples later as a thank you from a whisky sales lady, namely Anne?

Behold, the reignition of a passion for surgery. This had nothing to do with the whisky or any self-fulfilling gift; this was about the patient experience. It was moments like these that reminded me of my ambition to become a surgeon, or at least, to work in healthcare in any capacity. In that particular moment, I was doing a surgical procedure that brought me closer to my north star. But from where was my passion birthed?

Countless visits to general practitioners and specialists, multiple plausible diagnoses, random food restrictions, numerous calls from my school to my parents to pick me up and large volumes of medical notes groomed my curiosity. It all culminated in a diagnosis of epilepsy. All these things led me to take an interest in medicine and healthcare. In addition, I spent subsequent years reading my own x-ray films alongside doctors, blindly trying to make sense of electroencephalogram (EEG) reports, and intently studying the information insert that came with the anticonvulsant medicine I was prescribed.

I spent so much time in health service environments that I started to know their workflows and procedures. But the push to question and understand my own results presented graphically, pictorially or noted was a mere natural interest. I guess you could say it was my calling from that young age. With such interest, and growing up seeing my mum act as my nurse, the future was inevitable. But such curiosity was kept incubated for years while dealing with the more important phase in life: adolescence.

During those years of maturity, the political and economic outlook in my home country, Zimbabwe, had progressively declined. This was the major factor that started me thinking about migration, added to the fact that my older siblings had already taken the route of diaspora. Initially, I explored the possibility of migrating to Canada or the USA, and I received university offers to study chemical engineering and computer science, respectively. But, ultimately, I chose the UK because of the proximity to family. At 21 years of age, I arrived in the UK and spent the next twelve months trying to figure out what to do next.

What I didn't realise (and a lot after me) is that, as an immigrant, the way your life shapes up after arriving in a new country is a reflection of the people around you. It is like the African saying, "It takes a village to raise a child." In the end, the voices around me proved too loud to ignore. Needless to say, the idea of going to nursing school seemed not to be *an* option but the *only* option. Luckily for me, in comparison to others who arrived at the same time, I was surrounded by open-minded and knowledgeable people, and I knew my options were beyond nursing. But the calling of being a surgeon supported this nursing idea, and in my mind, it would be a cost-effective way to get through medical school.

At one point, I almost withdrew from the admission process as my application hit a red flag: the government was stopping the funding of immigrants onto the course. So, I thought to myself, "Can I afford this, having been in diaspora for only a year?" After some enquiries up the chain, the university confirmed that I could be admitted and would be fully funded. The relief from receiving that decision was like the moment when one grasps for air after having been under water for a while.

Due to my early childhood diagnosis of epilepsy, the next hurdle, as part of the admission process, was to undertake neurological tests. Fortunately, I passed, and a line was drawn under that diagnosis. From that point on, my diagnosis was changed to febrile convulsions. A lot of life's journey rests heavily upon a few smaller factors, and if I had failed that test, or if I had not received funding, my whole future would have been derailed.

In Zimbabwe, I had completed an economics degree, so when I embarked on my nursing studies, I assumed that the experience of university in the UK would be just like it was back home. The unknown was how the different culture and set-up would shock and turn idealism to realism.

Walking into a lecture room of 250 classmates to find I was one of only three immigrants, who were also Africans, was not expected or easy to digest. Nevertheless, we were accepted and made very welcome. In fact, I couldn't have asked for a warmer Scottish reception, and I believe I left Scotland as an honorary Scotsman.

My very first placement was also my first time in a nursing home. The team was welcoming and supportive, but cultural perspectives presented a challenge. In Zimbabwe, family members take care of their elderly until their last breath, but now I was learning how UK families place their elderly into nursing homes. I had mixed feelings as well as certain perceptions about the lack of empathy and love of the British for placing their loved ones in these environments. This was, by far, the biggest cultural shock to my system. But, after working in the home and seeing the support residents received from their families, I realised it was not so much a societal issue as it was a service opportunity.

In gearing up for the final placement of the course, all students were asked to select three preferred placements, and then we waited nervously to find out where we had been allocated. The waiting game took me right back to the anxiety of whether or not I would be funded in the first place. However, I was honoured to be assigned to my first choice, which was a surgical unit. Hence, I was placed in the general surgery and colorectal unit, where I met and treated Anne.

All of my childhood feelings towards medicine and surgery came flooding back and culminated into enthusiasm and eagerness to learn everything I could during that 13-week placement. With the greatest of teams, I was treated no less than any other student, and I felt I received equal opportunities. In my eyes, the unit had a brilliant manager who ran the team well. Having the unit deputy manager as my mentor meant that feedback on my performance was literally always in the manager's ear, and she took a liking for my work ethic.

A few weeks into the placement, one of the part-time nurses announced their retirement. Within a short space of time, the unit manager invited me to a meeting, and I was offered the post that was becoming vacant. Sadly, I had to decline, as immigration rules meant I needed a full-time role to gain a work permit. For a moment, I had forgotten I was even an immigrant because, amongst that team, I was one of them.

Fast forward a few weeks, and I was called to another meeting where the unit manager informed me that another nurse was retiring due to poor health. The retirement was not official, but I could have the job once confirmed, and I am happy to say, this time, it was a full-time job! Only leaving the unit six years later, it is safe to say I made the right choice.

During that time, I did see some internal and external opportunities pass me by. For example, I was never put forward to attend training to be a student mentor; nurses who joined the unit after me were put forward instead. Actually, the students enjoyed working with me and being taught by me, and when the new unit manager heard about it, I was often allocated students to mentor. But this was still not enough to be put forward to have the training to do what I was already doing. I confronted the practice education facilitator about it, and the response was that they never thought I would stay long, that I would move on very soon. My only response was, "Very soon has taken six years so far!"

Two years into that job, I did take the liberty of looking around for other jobs. I found there were numerous opportunities across Scotland and England. One application was accepted at a big hospital in London for a job in their intensive care unit (ICU). On invitation, I attended a three-part assessment and interview process. I was impressed with the hospital, and the recruitment team were impressed by my interview, and I was offered the job on the same day. Sometimes, when things are going so well, one can forget their situation. I accepted the offer, and then came the communication from their human resources department: ICU jobs were not on the Home Office job shortage list; therefore, it would be difficult for them to support me in getting a work permit.

Oh, the journey of an immigrant! The skills and knowledge were present on my part, but a simple technicality made all the difference, and it all came tumbling down. Attempts were made by the hospital to recruit me onto a non-specialist ward with the aim of getting my work permit and then transferring me to ICU. But that failed, and the door to the ICU job closed permanently.

All I could see ahead of me in nursing were closed doors, and this was compounded by the missed career progression opportunities. However, this motivated me to pivot my career and embark on a Master's degree in business administration. After a lot of self-discovery and consulting, I ditched the dream of medical school altogether. Now, the plan was to harness my nursing skills and experience with my business management training to feed my ambition and open new doors.

The deeper I progressed with my postgraduate studies, the more my observations became clear regarding process improvements that needed to be made at ward level. Remembering back to the nursing processes in Zimbabwe, I realised that the UK processes were much more developed, but I still saw gaps in the efficiency of them. The amount of material and time waste by nurses, the ineffective management of staff by ward managers (that hindered team bonding and productivity), and the lack of daily visual workflows that could be engineered for improved service provision, were but a few areas visible to my eye.

Coincidentally, at one point, the introduction of management consultants in English NHS hospitals made its way to my hospital in Scotland. The consultancy was focussed on introducing 'Lean' management principles, and each ward taking part in the pilot was asked to select two members of staff to represent the ward. I stood by as other members of staff were chosen ahead of me. Yet, I understood the principles because I was studying them! To add salt to the wound, I was studying my operations management module at the time and had already covered 'Lean'. My colleagues queried why I was not part of this initiative, as they also felt I was better placed to assist. To this day, I do not know how the selection was made, what the criteria were, or how validated it was. Although I tried not to make it an issue, this was a recurring effect of being a nurse in diaspora. Whether I would have brought much success will never be known now, but certainly, a skilled manager would have considered better the selection criteria. Was I expecting too much of my ward manager? Well, it certainly made me question the ability of a ward 'sister/matron' to be a 'manager'. Subsequently, it served as the topic of my dissertation.

With my mentoring hat on, would I recommend nursing in the United Kingdom? Of course! This position assumes the recommendation is given to someone with a keen interest in nursing and not someone who wants to train just for the sake of it. Simply experiencing a working environment in a western environment brings about growth. Exposure cannot be understated, more so for individuals from third-world countries where knowledge sharing, media and access are regulated beyond reasonable needs. Nursing in Europe has a totally different dimension, and it redefines the role of a nurse in a big way. The role proffers greater ownership and authority in the delivery of needed healthcare to enhance the patient pathway. It's a dimension that would prove very empowering within the Zimbabwean health service, for both nurses and patients.

My positive recommendation is based on not fearing the diaspora effects. These are just causes for determination. No environment offers no challenges, and challenges are meant to keep us striving for more and better.

Career progression is available in the UK. Let no immigrant nurse deny you your ambition based on the sentiment that "it will not work". Each individual should write their own destiny. Once written, it is up to them to walk the path and turn a dream into a reality.

In my opinion, the NHS is the best health service in the world and equates in size to Fortune 500 companies. Why not be a component of such a giant? Like any other organisation, innovation is about continuous improvement. What was best practice a year ago, can already have points of opportunity for improvement today.

My journey started with the dream of being a surgeon, but I will never regret staying in nursing. Everything I experienced was worth it, from the work I carried out and the patient experiences I was a part of … to the lives I worked to save with colleagues and the families we supported when lives were lost. These experiences highlighted my worth and stimulated my hunger for a bigger challenge. So here I am, the economics student turned immigrant nurse, turned operations manager, turned CRM (Customer Relationship Management) administrator, turned medical software architect. This is my story.

2

My Passion for Nursing

I am from the beautiful island of St. Vincent and the Grenadines in the Caribbean. I am the fourth of nine children and was born at home in a very small village called Rose Bank, located on the leeward side of the country. My siblings and I were raised by both parents in a humble Christian home.

My passion for nursing started at the tender age of five. I still have fond memories of how I would care for all the animals we owned. As I grew older, the focus moved from animals to people, especially my relatives and those with whom I had a close bond, which included Mrs Haper, one of the villager's most treasured residents. I often took the time to visit this elderly lady, who was about 90 years old at the time.

Mrs Haper was a midwife in her younger years, and many, including myself, were delivered by her skilful hands. She taught me many practical things, such as how to use hot water with very clean white cloths and what herbal medicines help with particular ailments. Therefore, whenever anyone in my house felt unwell, I was the first to run and gather various leaves to make medicine. For fevers, baby bush was boiled and then used in a bath; For headaches, the same baby bush wrapped in a cloth and tied onto the head worked miracles; For stomach pain, leaves from lime trees were used as a remedy. Many in my neighbourhood called me "Nursie". I can only smile at how simple these things were, but equally, they were fundamentally important to the career path I chose.

When I was 12, my family moved to the city, and my passion faded slightly as I tried to adapt to a new environment. Nevertheless, I remained a caring teenager. After finishing my secondary school education, I enrolled at the community college to study law and business. My grades were good, but I soon realised that it was not my calling. So, by the middle of the first year, I quit and signed up for nursing school instead. It was the best decision I have ever made. The course was challenging, but I dedicated myself to the studies, and the reward was great.

In 2008, I graduated and moved to Barbados, where I first worked at the Queen Elizabeth Hospital for two years, mainly as a surgical nurse. Subsequently, I worked as a general nurse at Bayview Hospital for two years. My experiences at both places were beautiful. I saw people at their worst and then at their best. The most amazing feeling in the world is when a patient is grateful enough to say thank you. I met many families, both local and international, and seeing their joy at their loved ones being cared for in a safe and friendly environment was one of the most satisfying parts of my role.

It wasn't always laughter and smiles. Whenever a patient died on my shift, I would wait around to speak to the family, even if my shift had finished – especially if they had not been there when their loved one passed. Most people are comforted by knowing their loved ones died peacefully. I always believed that, as that patient's nurse, I owed the family an explanation of my patient's last few hours. Nursing is hard work; it requires passion, care and dedication. However, it is extremely rewarding.

During my time at Bayview Hospital, I got married. My husband was in the Royal Navy and wanted me to join him in England. At first, I was hesitant to leave my job, for I had heard from others how difficult it was to get registered with the Nursing and Midwifery Council (NMC) in the UK. So, I decided to stay in Barbados for another year and complete my dialysis training, which I did at SILS Dialysis (a renal care facility). The patients and I had a very good nurse-patient relationship. Creating diet plans with my patients was the most challenging part of the job.

Leaving that unit was extremely hard as my patients had all come to trust me, and establishing that trust did not happen overnight. The ones who didn't like other nurses setting up their machines were not happy if I was off sick for one day! I missed working with them.

In September of 2013, I arrived in England. We lived in the South West for eighteen months, where I worked as a healthcare assistant (HCA) in a nursing home. I appreciated the breath-taking views and the wide range of food. But I didn't realise that many struggles lay ahead.

Before I could even register with the NMC, I had to pass the IELTS exam (International English Language Testing System). The NMC's reasoning for the test was to protect patients from miscommunication. However, I came from an English-speaking country! It took me about three years, after many disappointing results and sleepless nights, to pass the exam. Then it was brought to my attention that people from the European Union were not required to take the test, even though their first language was not English. At first, I was angry and decided not to bother with the IELTS anymore. I knew that I was not a failure; I believed in my strength and intelligence. Yet, because of my geographical origin, I was not granted the same opportunity as others.

The worst part of my job was translating medical information into everyday language for the patients. I often wondered why the NMC was protecting patients from my English and communication skills! Especially when patients were at a greater risk at the hands of those who spoke very little English but were never dealt with so robustly and brought under such scrutiny. Sometimes, I would just contemplate how unfair life could be. I was happy as an HCA, helping those who need care, but deep down, I was never fulfilled. I knew I could contribute more at an advanced level.

Oh, the joy of helping the elderly. Getting my residents ready for their day was the top priority. A few ladies would specifically request that I aided them in getting dressed just so they could have their makeup done. It was fun. Working at that nursing home showed me exactly what the circle of life is like. When I looked at photos of our residents in their youth, it was hard to believe that they were the same person. The hardest part of the job was putting my nursing skills aside, for that was not my role. Though difficult to do, I managed. At times, I became homesick, and all I wanted to do was to return home. There I could practice my nursing skills.

A year and a half later, my husband and I moved to another city, and I got a job as a Band 2 HCA at a hospital for rheumatic diseases. I met some amazing people there who encouraged me not to give up. And so, I tried the IELTS several more times before I passed. I was over the moon with excitement. I felt like I had finally made it! I started my registration process with the NMC, and I was also successful in an application for a Band 4 HCA role at the hospital.

As a Band 4 HCA, I had more autonomy to use my nursing skills, and with the necessary education and training offered by the hospital, I was extremely confident in my new role. I passed the computer-based test that the NMC recommended as the first stage of registration. I sent off all my paperwork and then started studying for the objective structured clinical examination (OSCE), which is the final exam prior to registration with the NMC.

The sleepless nights started again, but my confidence had been boosted, and I was determined to pass. However, I received little guidance from the NMC and just as little from the university where I sat my OSCE. I found the content of study materials very limited for they were not specific to the marking criteria, and I was left having to figure out what was expected of me.

I have now taken the OSCE twice and not passed. Both times, I felt crushed and wanted to call it quits.

But I love nursing!

So, despite all the challenges and set-backs, I decided to start a new application with the NMC. I plan to get my nursing PIN, regardless of the struggles. I am willing to work hard and educate myself by any means necessary. This time, though, I have a back-up plan, so if I'm disappointed again, it won't hurt as much.

As an aspiring registrant with the NMC, I would recommend that nurses' skills be tested in an environment that reflects the real nature of nursing. Anyone can show up to an OSCE and meet all the criteria, but it's on the wards, at the clinics, in the GP surgeries etc. that true nursing qualities can be demonstrated. That's where passion is seen.

Even though the journey has been tough for me, I would encourage others to work in the UK for several reasons. First, everyone has different circumstances, and I would not want anyone to think that they will automatically encounter the same difficulties as me. Second, being a nurse in the UK can lead to endless career development possibilities. Third, those who wish to later return home will do so with much knowledge that will benefit the populace of their country of origin in numerous ways. So, if one of my friends or colleagues from the Caribbean asks for my opinion about being a nurse in the UK, my answer to them will be, "How resilient are you?" If the answer is, "Very," then I will encourage them to take the step.

If I was to take this journey again, I personally would not come to the UK. If my husband could be relocated to the Caribbean, I will definitely be happy. My career went on pause, not because I intended it to, but because of rules. And if looked at carefully, one can see the flaws in those rules. For three years, I struggled to pass the IELTS. It's not an ordinary English exam; it's more of a points-based skills test. How can the NMC truly want to protect the British public from miscommunication by imposing an English exam on a person whose first language is English but not for people who can't speak or have limited English? I am happy that the NMC has changed this rule and new NMC applicants don't need to take the IELTS if they come from an English-speaking country. I believe that this will act as a precursor to increasing numbers of nurses joining the UK register.

However, my struggle continues. My application was already being processed by the NMC when they changed the rule, so it didn't apply to me, and when my IELTS expired, I had to re-take it. Now, the issue is proving my residence in an English-speaking country. This is despite having lived and worked in the UK since 2013. I have all the evidence – letters, bank records etc.

– but the NMC's system doesn't recognise them. Sometimes, I wonder how ridiculous the systems can get!! It's very frustrating and disappointing. I could have been working as a registered nurse by now, helping the NHS with its chronic nursing staff shortages. Instead, I am still stuck in the system.

3

Nursing in the Middle East

Even as a teenager, I knew that I wanted to work in healthcare. I was not sure, however, whether I wanted to be a paramedic or a nurse. At college, I was advised by a teacher to obtain a nursing qualification first and then later train as a paramedic, if I still wanted to. And so, I applied to do nursing at university. At the time, students had the option of qualifying with either a diploma or a degree. I chose the former. Very soon, I was enjoying my training, and I forgot all about my dreams of becoming a paramedic.

After finishing my diploma, I worked as a registered nurse for a total of six years in the UK. I was quite settled in my role, but around the fifth year, I started to yearn for a new challenge, and it took another year before all my plans fell into place.

My hope for something different led me to consider working abroad. I researched the benefits of doing so and found that Saudi Arabia offered great benefits for foreign workers. I then checked out several nursing recruitment agencies that could help me with the process of seeking a job in diaspora. Having spoken to only one nurse who had worked in the Middle East before, I was truly relying on the agency I chose, as well as the material I continued to source online.

The agency asked me to provide them with specific information about my nursing experience and skills, including the types of patients I had worked with and any areas of speciality. Next, I had an interview with the agency via Skype, in which they asked me direct medical questions and gave me scenarios to respond to. For the rest of that day, I waited patiently, and when they rang me back, they confirmed that they had a job for me on a surgical unit.

Following this, the process seemed to speed up. In reality, though, it took several months just to sort the paperwork. A lady from the agency was selected as my point of contact for any information regarding the process of application. She was friendly and made everything much less daunting and quite straightforward.

First, I applied for a working visa. Then I was sent a ten-page employment contract to read and sign – it contained quite a few pages translated from Arabic that explained the Islamic laws of the country. I had to sign to say I fully understood that breaking those laws would result in imprisonment or even death, depending on the type of misdemeanour. I knew I would not be breaking any of the Saudi laws (such as bringing alcohol or drugs to the country), so I signed it. I must admit, though, that a part of me did wonder what I was getting myself into.

Once the contract was signed, I then registered for my Iqama, which is a work permit card for foreign workers who live in Saudi Arabia. It has to be renewed yearly and is essential for certain things, such as purchasing a SIM card, opening a bank account, gaining access to the internet, travelling out of the country, booking tickets and hospital visits.

Some of the other things required for my application included: Having my qualifications and nursing PIN notarised in the UK then sent to the Royal Embassy of Saudi Arabia Cultural Bureau to be verified; Gaining a police clearance; Undergoing a full medical examination, involving a chest x-ray and blood tests; Proving my employment in the UK.

As the time approached for my new adventure, I moved out of my flat and put some of my belongings in storage, as I was planning to return after one year, or sooner if things did not work out. Little did I know that I would not be returning for four years. While waiting for everything to be finalised, I stayed with my mum. When I showed her my contract conditions, she was concerned and asked if I really wanted to go. But I knew I would be ok because I didn't intend to break any of the rules.

In total, the whole application process took six months. Finally, half a year later, after all the back and forth from the post office to mail my documents by special delivery, it arrived: my ticket to Saudi Arabia! It was finally real! The following day, I received an email from the lady at the agency checking that my ticket had arrived safely and asking me to keep in touch. She even attempted to contact someone already working in Saudi to see if we could meet each other when I arrived and was settled.

Upon arriving on Arab soil, I was met at the airport by a hospital representative who was holding a clipboard with the names of the newly employed staff who needed to be collected. I was then taken to the compound where I would be living. I arrived at the 'villa' (as it was called), but nobody was home. I looked around the villa, trying to guess what my new housemate would be like. She had left a welcome note to say that she was at work and that I could help myself to anything in the fridge. I felt more at ease, and I proceeded to my room, where I had been left a gift from the hospital – it was a box (like a lunchbox) containing food and drink items.

The next day, I went to the hospital for the start of the two-week orientation, and on my way, I bumped into a group of female nurses. Long story short, they had met randomly and were all in the same position as me, having travelled individually to Saudi for work without knowing anyone else in the country. As you can imagine, we had a lot to talk about, and we traded stories about where we came from, why we had come to Saudi and what our recruitment process was like. We quickly became friends, and we still are to this day.

During the orientation, the hospital management told all the new starters about the country and its cultural customs, and they gave us a list of some useful Arabic words to learn. We were also given an orientation pack, which detailed useful information such as emergency contact numbers, a map of the hospital, and the bus (coach) timetables. We were then taken to different areas of the hospital to apply for our ID card (Iqama) and set up a bank account. We also registered with the Saudi Arabian nursing council and were put on a 3-month probation period. Following this, we were each shown to the units where we would be working and formally introduced to the staff. I felt very grateful and lucky that another nurse started alongside me on the surgical unit. It helped immensely because we were able to support each other through the transition of working in a foreign country.

Most of the nursing agencies had detailed the types of feelings we might encounter when living and working in a different country. They were trying to prepare us to deal with the emotions that arise from certain situations, such as being away from family and 'culture shock'. The transition period was not as hard as I first imagined it would be, and the frustrations I felt were only minor (such as how long it took to set up my bank account, then having to keep going back to check if money transfers had gone through because the process was quite slow). I overcame these feelings quickly, though, and it definitely helped to have friends around who were going through the same things. Plus, we soon met other nurses who had been in Saudi for much longer, and they were able to offer helpful advice.

On the surgical unit, my nursing skills were assessed, and I learned about the hospital policies and protocols. I shadowed a lovely nurse and mentor who had worked at the hospital for more than ten years. She was so welcoming and patient. Sadly, she passed away due to a health complication while working there. My nursing colleagues and I were devastated, as she was such a huge part of our lives. Her goal had been to work until retirement and the return to her country of origin to enjoy the remainder of her life.

I enjoyed looking after the different patients, though the language barrier was frustrating at the beginning. Not everyone spoke English fluently, and not being able to understand what my patients were saying made me feel inadequate as a nurse. My colleagues often became interpreters, and I used a notebook to record basic words. After about six months, I knew enough Arabic to get by on the ward, but I still needed the assistance of my colleagues for trickier words and phrases.

By the time I was getting to grips with the language, I was also feeling settled in Saudi. Nursing, I found, was comparable to the UK in terms of safety checks, medicines used, hygiene care, and pre-op and post-op care. The only major differences were in the structure and policies. Policy-wise, there was a lot of emphasis on safety, especially medication safety. Thus, all medications were pre-mixed at the hospital pharmacy, which made it easier and faster to administer drugs, and I found that this method was effective in minimising errors. When it came to blood products, the administration was checked by three different people, and all three had to sign the relevant forms.

Initially, the hospital used a paper system for all of our data, but after two years, it changed to a computerised system. I very much enjoyed using the latter, for it was easy to use, and it contained everything we needed, including the doctors' notes, which meant us nurses no longer needed to decipher illegible handwriting! On our unit, the new system meant that patients consented to surgery using an iPad. They would sign it, and the doctor and nurses would witness their consent and also sign it.

Being a nurse of colour in the Middle East was a different experience. A lot of patients and their relatives or visitors could not believe that I was from the UK, some responding along the lines of, "No, that cannot be true!" This caused much amusement to my colleagues! It was all quite funny, really, with one patient insisting that I was from Sri Lanka!

Another aspect of living abroad that I enjoyed was learning about a different culture. The Saudi culture is completely unlike my own and is considered by many in the first world as dated. For example, women are not allowed to drive (though, this law was changed in 2018) and females need permission from their husband, father or brother to travel outside of the country.

But, of course, not every Saudi family shares these views. I worked alongside a Saudi female who had a very open family dynamic. She never covered her face, only her hair in a modest fashion. She informed me that she could travel wherever she pleased and often went abroad on holiday with friends. I was pleasantly surprised by her ability to be so open about her life. I asked her how she felt about Saudi stereotyping, such as having to have an arranged marriage. She said that she had told her family that if she doesn't find a suitable husband, she is planning to adopt a child and raise him or her alone.

I worked with a few other Saudi females, and I was happy to find that a lot of them had quite independent minds, all the while maintaining respect for their culture and country. Meeting people who grew up in Saudi, people I would probably never have met in the UK, has given me some great memories.

There will always be negative aspects of a country, and in Saudi Arabia, I found it in their use of maids and nannies. At work, I noted how many families utilise foreigners for these roles, commonly females from the Philippines, Kenya, Ethiopia or Sudan. At the shopping malls, I saw despondent-looking maids trailing behind their bosses, or as they call them, 'sponsors'. I worked with a lady who had been in Saudi for at least 20 years, and she told me some stories about how horribly maids and nannies were treated. Women, generally from poor countries, would come to Saudi with the promise of a fantastic job as a receptionist, only to arrive and find themselves trapped in a room with ten other women. Then Saudi people, generally men, would come and pick one to work as their maid or nanny. Often, the women were stripped of their travel documents for 'processing' or some other made-up reason. Then they would work for free, pretty much 24 hours a day, sometimes getting woken up in the middle of the night to carry out household duties. Without a phone or access to one, these women were alone and unable to contact their families.

I cannot say that every maid or nanny is mistreated. But, alarmingly, many stories confirm this does happen. It disheartened me and made me question whether it was ethical for me to continue working there. But, of course, not every

Saudi family is the same, and I have heard positive stories of maids going on lovely holidays with families and being treated decently and humanely.

Overall, I am truly grateful for having had the opportunity to work in the Middle East. While there, I managed to save money, which I used wisely on my return to the UK. To those who wish to nurse in the Middle East, I would certainly recommend it, but I also advise to do your research first.

I have no regrets of choosing nursing as a career choice, and I look forward to what the future has in store for me.

4

A Profession or a Calling?

At the young age of 20, I left the African shores to further my education and career in Europe. In Zimbabwe, I had worked at a bank and started an accounting course, so my plan was to continue with my studies overseas. Arriving in England and realising that it was not that easy came as a big shock. Education was expensive, and I would need to work while studying in order to survive.

I couldn't afford to study accounting, so I started working. I managed to secure a few cleaning jobs, but my main job was at a nursing home, which came as an even bigger shock to my system! Nothing had prepared me for looking after old people and assisting them with their daily living. It had never entered my mind that I would need such a job. Naïvely, I thought I would easily find myself a good job in an English office or bank. It turned out that I was fooling myself!

Initially, I found the work challenging, for I was young and ambitious, and it was not my dream to work with old people. But after some time, I began to enjoy my time at the care home, and I came to value the old people I helped on an almost daily basis.

A year later, I made the crucial decision to pursue a career in nursing instead of accounting. I was already nursing people, so it made it sense from that perspective. But, also, studying would make it easier for me to renew my visa, and nursing offered the added bonus of zero tuition fees and a bursary. So, it made financial sense as well.

I applied to a local university and was extremely pleased when I was accepted. They gave me a place on a course for mental health nursing, but I had no idea what that really meant, as I thought nursing was nursing. Coming from Zimbabwe where mental health issues were not spoken about much, it was all very new to me.

I felt more at ease, though, when the course started and I met some fellow Zimbabweans. And ultimately, I grew to enjoy mental health nursing! On the first day of my first ever placement, however, I almost regretted taking on this new venture, for I walked into a psychiatric unit for elderly patients to the sound of screaming and shouting. I comforted and reassured myself that I could handle whatever lay ahead for I had worked with older people before.

My role was different from the nursing home, of course, because it involved more than just feeding and bathing the patients. As the days went by, I learned about the different psychiatric illnesses that beset the elderly, illnesses such as dementia. I also learned about the types of medications given and the best ways of helping suffering patients and their families.

My other placements gave me the experience of working within eating disorder units, challenging behaviour units, addiction centres, and the prison service. All of these areas were an eye-opener for me, and I learned a lot, even about myself.

Working on the eating disorder unit was definitely the most challenging of all my placements. At first, I could not understand why anyone would refuse to eat food. Coming from Africa, where poverty and shortage are rife, such behaviour is unheard of. An African friend of mine on the same placement asked to be transferred elsewhere; she, too, could not make sense of such illnesses when people in other nations are starving to death. Over time, though, I understood some of the reasons why people suffer from eating disorders, and I learned how to help these individuals feel better about themselves.

When I qualified, my first job was at a remand prison. My role entailed looking after prisoners with mental health issues and/or addictions. Prisons can be challenging places to work as a nurse because the job requires that one cares for people who have done bad things in society. But nurses are trained to always care and never judge, even in these kinds of situations. In fact, I came to appreciate that some of the prisoners committed crimes because of their mental illnesses.

I learned a lot about how and why one can end up addicted – and there are many reasons. Ultimately, it sparked an interest within me to work with people with drug and alcohol addictions. Some of the prisoners were the same age as me, and this helped me to relate to them, understand their challenges, and discuss with them the issues they were facing.

When my 2-year contract with the prison services came to an end, I started working for an agency, which meant I gained experience of working in different units and hospitals. A while later, a friend of mine recommended Ireland as a place to live and work; she said the living and working conditions were better than in England. And so, I moved and found a job in a mental health hospital.

On my first day, as I walked to the main administration office, all I could see were piles of incontinence pads on the window sills. Immediately, I worried, "Oh, I hope this is not a nursing home!" When I got to the office, the assistant director of nursing told me that I needed to go into town and get myself a white tunic uniform. In England, mental health nurses did not wear uniforms, so this news seemed to confirm my worst fears. Don't get me wrong, I love old people, but at this stage in my career, I wanted to work in adult acute mental health.

The next day, I returned in my white tunic and asked the manager what type of ward I would be working on. She explained that I would be working on different wards – the admission unit, the secure unit and the long-stay wards. She also explained that all nurses wore uniforms, which came as a huge surprise and relief for me, as I did not want to go back and work in nursing homes again.

For most of the first year, I worked in a secure unit with patients who exhibited challenging behaviours. Verbal and physical aggression was a daily occurrence, and self-harm was also quite common. The nurses spent much of their time transferring patients to a general hospital for x-rays and treatments, as the patients would often swallow foreign objects, such as cutlery, or they would cut their wrists with sharp objects. Every now and then, the nurses were moved to a different ward to have a break from that unit. It was our only saving grace, for that unit was not good for our own mental health. Staff would joke, saying, "Before you enter that unit, you need to bless yourself with holy water, for you don't know what you'll find or how the shift will go."

Working in Ireland was a bit different from working in England, but I enjoyed the experiences of both. Mental illness is the same regardless of the location, and this made it easy for me to move from one country to another. I discovered first-hand that nursing gave me the liberty of moving without the worry of finding a job. It's an ideal profession if one desires that kind of freedom. Nurses are required in every part of the world, and it is the one career that will always be necessary, no matter the economy of the nation.

I never forgot my passion for working with people with addictions, so once settled in Ireland, I did a degree in addiction counselling. Following this, whenever I worked in the hospital's admission unit and met patients with addiction problems, I was able to use the skills I had learned to help them.

After working at the hospital for about seven years, I applied for a clinical nurse manager position. I was successful, and I worked in that role for two years. It entailed working in community hostels and looking after patients with enduring mental health issues, most of whom had spent the majority of their lives in mental health institutes.

In 2016, I decided to return to university for a postgraduate course in mental health. This qualification enabled me to secure a job as a clinical nurse specialist, which is still my position today. Currently, I have a caseload of patients who suffer from different mental health problems. My role involves visiting people in their homes for assessment and support, and also empowering patients to play an active part in their own recovery.

I am very grateful for the opportunities I've had in my nursing career. I have managed to further my education and advance in my career, all with the support of my family. Nursing has given me so much pleasure as well as the freedom to travel anywhere in the world and embark on different projects.

Is nursing a profession or a calling for me? I can happily answer that nursing has become my calling. I am very passionate about what I do, and I love helping people feel better about themselves and helping them realise how special they are. To be able to work as a nurse, you have to be someone who loves people, which is why I say that it is a calling, not just a profession. Most nurses have to work long hours caring for other people, and this makes it a calling. To name but a few, some of the qualities I think one needs to be a nurse include: patience, care, compassion and consideration. Most importantly, though, it is essential for nurses to take time for themselves as well (self-care). My nursing job has allowed me to spend quality time with my family and live a comfortable life in diaspora, and I am truly grateful for that.

5

Life Isn't Always Rainbows and Butterflies

As it says in the Bible, *"Many are the plans in a person's heart, but it is the Lord's purpose that prevails."* (Proverbs 19:21, NIV).

Back during the time when I was still a student nurse, I planned my future based on the currency exchange. Yup, you read that right. Nursing in the Philippines is not purely passion-driven anymore; it has become a commodity, something that has international trade value. We were all competing and striving to attain that highly-prized "professional license", and to many of us, it was a ticket to the world.

Undeniably, the Philippines has carved itself a name for producing world-class qualified nurses who are highly sought after by many employers throughout the globe. It is a well-known fact that nurses from the Philippines are of high calibre (modesty aside). That's because, as a nation, we do everything with excellence; we are taught to do well and to always give our best effort in every circumstance.

But for me, I was planning where I would go based on how much money I could potentially make. I researched which country would give me the most value for the Philippine Peso (PHP). Was it the USD? AUD? BHD? AED?

At my graduation, more than one hundred students graduated alongside me, equating to over a hundred dreams, goals, desires and plans. I managed to finish at the top of my class. Was I special? One might think so. But after four years of studying, we were all in the same position of plodding on and burning the midnight candle to study for our licensure exam, which is equivalent in difficulty to America's NCLEX (National Council Licensure Examination). I managed to pass – goal achieved! I now had a small plastic card that said I was a qualified professional nurse. Now, the world was my oyster; I could go and work wherever I wanted and earn those currencies that my oblivious younger self day-dreamed about.

At the beginning of 2012, when I started to look for a job, the Philippines had over 200,000 unemployed nurses and an estimated 80,000 graduates each year coming. Wow! Talk about competition! "No matter," I thought, "for the world is big enough for all of us."

Before looking for a job overseas, however, I needed to gain experience of working in a hospital. Months and months passed by, and I wasn't able to find a paying job. The private, paying hospitals tended not to hire newly graduated nurses, so I succumbed to what everyone else was doing to get a job experience – I worked for free as a "volunteer nurse" at the local hospital. I volunteered for two and a half years, first working in paediatrics, then the emergency department. The whole time, I was desperately applying for jobs in the Middle East as well as revising for English exams for Australian jobs. I had to cover all my bases and lay the foundations for every eventuality. Still, after investing thousands and thousands of pesos, I was no closer to my goals.

Eventually, I got a job in the emergency department of a private hospital, but it paid very little, roughly 8000 PHP (est. £110 during those times) per month. It was barely enough to sustain my daily living, but it was still helpful for our family, for I was able to help out with the bills, reward myself in little ways and still not go hungry.

As a Christian and a firm believer that God cares for my wellbeing, I knew that His plans for my life were higher than mine. At that time, I could not even begin to comprehend everything that was ahead of me. Still, I continued my quest to work overseas, taking the IELTS exam twice in two years (the international English language testing system). Both times, my score was 0.5 points short on one aspect to qualify to apply for work in Australia (the requirement was 7 points in all four areas, and I achieved 6.5 in writing). I had always considered myself to be a good writer. Yet, for some reason, attaining a score of 7 proved to be elusive.

Then one fateful day, a message came from my uncle (Dad's cousin) in the United Kingdom, someone I had never even spoken to before. Somehow, he knew that I was a nurse, and he offered to help me get a job in a nursing home in the UK. I'd never really considered working in that part of the world, but this seemed to be a good chance presenting itself.

It did mean, however, that I had to pass the IELTS exam! At this point, I felt a little fed up, but this was too good of a chance to waste. So, I asked my family to help me fund another attempt. The exam cost roughly 19,000 PHP (approx. £260-290), which was a huge amount to waste if I failed again. That money could have purchased food to last for a good few months. But we risked it all for a small glimpse of greener pastures. On the day of the exam, I felt like I had the weight of the world on my shoulders. "It's now or never," I told myself. "I can't afford to waste any more money."

I prayed harder than ever, and by the grace of God, I passed with a mark of 7 points or higher in all four areas! I did it! I was over the moon! This was more than just an examination; it was my future *and* my family's future.

But instead of following my uncle's recommendation, I looked for a recruitment agency that was looking for nurses to work in hospitals. I applied, and in a matter of weeks, I had interviews, took more exams and processed papers to work in the United Kingdom (at that point, I didn't realise how badly the NHS needed nurses). I had previously had my eyes set on Australia or the United States since I have more family there, but the UK wasn't a bad deal! I mean, who doesn't know the UK, its royals, films and history? For a career-driven individual like me, its plethora of opportunities was a perfect fit. I could almost see the Queen! Haha!

In 2016, I departed from the Philippines and arrived in the UK, the farthest place from home I'd ever been. I was halfway across the world. Alone. Officially, my life was now my own, for I had left my whole life behind me. With roughly 40kg of luggage and £200, I couldn't imagine what would happen in diaspora. All I knew was that to get to where I wanted to be, I needed to strive hard and be prepared to make sacrifices. My heart was filled with a myriad of emotions: doubt, worry, joy, excitement and curiosity. It was a battlefield. But amidst the raging chaos of emotions, I clung to the simple thought deeply embedded in my heart, "God brought me here for a reason, and I know He will never leave me."

Both of my parents had cousins working in the UK, but I had never met them or even talked to them before. At the airport, I met four other nurses in my cohort from different parts of the Philippines. We travelled together to our shared accommodation that was provided by the hospital.

My aunt and uncle (the one who had contacted me initially) helped by buying us some essential stuff and giving us old plates and other pieces of crockery. One of my other aunts bought me some winter clothes and shoes. Oh, did I forget to mention that we arrived in February, the peak of winter, after coming from a 36° climate? Boy, did we freeze! And I wondered what had happened to most of the trees – why were they dead? The concept of four seasons had never occurred to me before. And why was it dark so early in the day? It wasn't difficult to understand why many people in the UK become depressed.

In the Philippines, I lived in a coastal region that was surrounded by mountains. We enjoyed good sunshine, sparkling beaches and beautiful sunsets that were seemingly painted by God Himself day-by-day. But now I was living in a small English town, where it was dreary and dark. By the end of the afternoon, one lost sight of people! It was freezing cold, so I didn't even want to go outside. "I am way outside of my comfort zone here, God! Why am I here?" screamed the thoughts in my head. But God replied with a gentle answer, "Trust in Me!"

We were given a visa after passing the first part of our exams, but we still needed to pass part two, which was the OSCE (observed structured clinical examination). The NHS Trust, however, had to get what they paid for, so while studying and training for the exam, we were also working as Band 3 healthcare assistants. They were making us squeeze studying and training within a full rota.

When we received our placements, I was assigned to an acute medical ward. "Wow!" I thought to myself. Even though I didn't get a placement on A&E, which I thought I might have due to my background, this seemed close enough to my niche. I have never been so wrong! "Still," I thought to myself, "I'm here to work hard and represent the hundreds of thousands of nurses considerably less fortunate than me. I am employed in a hospital in the United Kingdom, and it's still better than what I had at home." Or was it? Back home (modesty aside again), I was a respected and established nurse, well-regarded by my peers, superiors, subordinates, patients and their families. In the UK, I was a nobody, an outsider, a newcomer and a novice.

At the start of my first day of work, I felt overwhelmed by what I would encounter in a new workplace with new equipment, new protocols, new policies, new workmates and new kinds of patients. I had never worked with Europeans or British people before. Questions rapidly flooded my mind, "Are they fun? Are they serious? Are they demanding? Strict? Sensible? Efficient? Smart?" I took a big breath and got on with it.

I focused on absorbing as much information as I could. Thankfully, I am a quick learner, so I soon got used to everything and everyone. I became especially fond of tea breaks! I had never worked in a place where the management cared so much about staff wellbeing. When working in the emergency department back home, I used to have a spoonful of my lunch at the reception table, attend to an incoming emergency, then manage another spoonful later that day, then just completely forget about food until the end of my shift. Sometimes, I'd forget to even take a toilet break! I got used to the fact that patients came first to the detriment of self. But in the UK, I found there is more balance. Patients *do* come first, but staff are given the space to invest in their own wellbeing. I appreciated the fact that I could say 'no' if I was overburdened, and I appreciated being recognised as a human who is also in need of care.

When the time for my OSCE arrived, I experienced another bout of emotional and mental chaos. But this time, I was more determined. I thought to myself, "I've come this far already. There is no way God is going to fail me now, so I just need to do my best."

All the hours and late nights of studying paid off … three days after taking the exam, I received an email informing me that I had passed! I did it! Soon after, I received my nursing PIN number and became an officially registered nurse in the United Kingdom.

Weeks and months passed. I worked very hard, and I worked a lot of extra hours. I earned enough money to pay off my debts back home as well as sustain myself in the UK and my family in the Philippines. I even had extra money to travel around Europe and to purchase whatever I wanted or needed. My hard work, knowledge and skills impressed my peers and my superiors.

For the first time ever, I had complete control over the outcomes of my life, but due to my cultural and familial obligations, I was also responsible for other people. Coming to England was supposed to be a move to a greener pasture. But as they say, "It's not always greener on the other side." Working away from my family, my girlfriend (I had a long-distance relationship then), my friends and my comfort zone was excruciatingly lonely. Yes, I could buy all the latest gadgets and gizmos I wanted, I could travel around Europe, I could eat whatever food I fancied, and I could do anything I wanted. But none of these things filled the loneliness I felt. Yes, I had friends, and I lived with fellow Filipinos (who were basically my family), but it was not the same.

One day I found myself feeling completely overwhelmed. My family back home had a huge financial setback. I was exhausted and fed-up from working so many hours. My relationship was strained due to the distance, and we broke up. My family thought that my life was better since I was earning more, and they looked to me every time they were in need. Don't get me wrong, I love my family, and I would do anything for them – I was already doing everything I could to save money to help them further.

All the different pressures added up, and I was miserable.

If I could go back in time and talk to myself when I was a student, I would say that sometimes it's not worth it. I had thought that working abroad would be the highlight of my career, that all the years of sacrifice and studying would be worth it because of the money. But at this low point, I realised that there is no place on earth like home! I was happier when I was earning less back home than in the UK with more. I never thought it would happen to me, but I was in a state of depression. The world felt like it was wasting away before me, that all there was in front of me was suffering.

But I did not falter in front of depression. I retaliated. I prayed more, worshipped God more, I spoke with friends and family more. I wasn't about to dig a deep hole and bury myself in it. I realised I wasn't alone: I had God, I had my family, and I had very good friends, one of whom is now my girlfriend!

Life isn't always full of rainbows and butterflies, but it's not always full of pain and suffering, either. There is joy in suffering and misery in abundance. Every person gets to choose how they will view and respond to life's situations.

My journey is still in its early chapters. I've worked hard, but I've also learned to take care of myself and value my relationships. It is wise to help others, but not at the cost of one's own wellbeing.

There is no point in the blind guiding the blind; we have to be kind to others but more so to ourselves. Earning more is not the solution to having a successful life. Success is achieved by learning to value what's really important, being content with what we are given and striving to be better versions of ourselves.

6

Therapeutic Nursing

———————

The experiences we go through in life are not supposed to make us bitter but leave us better.

Making the decision to leave the shores of Africa was one of the most difficult and painful decisions my husband and I have ever made. But it was also among the most crucial ones, and we made it in the prime of our lives.

We were in the same position as countless fellow countrymen and women who were making the same decision due to the economic crisis that loomed over our country at the time. Their choices were the validation we needed. However, I don't believe any of us made the decision lightly. Doom and gloom were the only things on the horizon in Zimbabwe. Hence, many jumped at the slightest chance of a new life elsewhere. We all wanted to fulfil our individual dreams and provide hope for the generations after us.

Our own diaspora journey started in the late 90s. We were recently married and had a new-born baby. The birth of our son brought a massive change to our lives, but we also felt the huge responsibility we held as parents.

When we initially discussed and assessed Zimbabwe's situation, we had two viable options, both of which presented us with a degree of risk. On the one hand, we could have stayed, believing that things would get better with time – but the risk was that the state of affairs would further deteriorate and we would no longer be able to leave the country. On the other hand, emigrating offered us the prospect of a hopeful future – but the risk was that we would be chartering into the unknown and unfamiliar, without even the promise of a job on the other end. Ultimately, we chose the second option. For us, it was time to do something radically different to pursue our dreams.

After arriving in the UK on our six-month visitor's visas, my husband was offered a place at university to further his accounting degree, but the fees required were such a huge stumbling block. If we'd had that kind of money, we could have easily facilitated our return home for a much more comfortable life. With that in mind, we went back to the drawing board in search of the next bright idea, always keeping an open mind to see the bigger picture.

Months later, and faced with the imminent expiration of our visitor's visas, we sought advice from family and friends. They recommended training as nurses, for it meant we would be supported fully in the financial sense.

And so, my journey of nursing started soon after. Actually, through a series of misfortunate events, both my husband and I were presented with the opportunity to study nursing. But that is a story for another day, one that I would love to get off my chest. But, for now, why nursing?

Attaining a place to study nursing meant a green route for obtaining a visa and less complication when extending one's stay in the country. For us, it was a means to an end, as we never saw ourselves working in this field. We had often shared stories about what we aspired to do in life, and nursing was never on the agenda.

Our family and friends were right about the perks, though. The 'package' included a bursary to cover expenses, including accommodation and food for the three of us. Really, it was a no-brainer; once we were offered places, we quickly accepted. I was so grateful for this opportunity to study at university, and the most phenomenal thing was that I would study with my husband. It was a humbling experience for me to study with him, for he was an accountant back home, accomplished already in his career. Plus, in Zimbabwe, it's unheard of for a man to be a nurse. Yet, he chose to study nursing with me. Both of us were determined to do what it took to achieve our goals and prove ourselves in this new profession.

Nursing was an eye-opener for me, and through it, I have learned many invaluable lessons. The foremost of which is that I saw nursing to be parallel to parenting, for both necessitate showing care and concern, and aiding someone else while they're helpless in their situation.

Watching patients recover and go on to live a full life, especially those who came into my care in great need, has been the most rewarding part of my career. Being able to play a part in facilitating their journey to recovery has been truly priceless. Florence Nightingale once said, *"I am of certain convinced that the greatest heroes are those who do their duty in the daily grind of domestic affairs whilst the world whirls as a maddening dreidel."*

The content of our class training was but a mere drop in the ocean compared to what I learned on placements and later on the job. Nursing is not an exhaustive subject where one can learn everything at college or university and graduate thinking,

"I possess all the knowledge I need." During my time of training, I diligently applied myself to all aspects of theoretical studies, but my most valuable lessons were learned through the practical application of nursing on our placements. On the wards, not only could I put into practice what I had learned in class, but I was also provided with plenty of opportunities to learn new things. I quickly realised that I learned more in practice than in theory, so I volunteered to do all sorts of jobs, and I thoroughly enjoyed each and every placement.

Naturally, I am a good communicator and genuinely like to meet people and talk. Others argue that I am nosey! However, communication is a vital tool in my specialist area of mental health. One of my mentors always said, "Listen more than you talk, and everything else will fall into place." This was another great lesson for me, for, at our core, each of us seeks to be listened to, to be understood, and to be validated. And one can multiply this need for those who are hurting, distressed or suffering, and even more so when they lack clarity and peace.

Having been trained in such a simplistic yet profound way, that most issues can be resolved by addressing the basic human needs (according to Maslow's hierarchical model), I began to reflect on the healthcare in Zimbabwe. I noticed that a disconnect exists between the models and beliefs taught and the way that healthcare is actually facilitated and delivered on the ground.

I believe that the emphasis in Zimbabwean nursing schools is more practical than theoretical, but throughout, the teaching is very sound. As a result, the country has produced high-quality nurses who excel in many countries across the globe, upholding strong work ethics and occupying top posts of leadership. However, I sincerely believe there remains a vast gap in their knowledge in terms of communication and bedside manner.

I have encountered a fair share of Zimbabwean professionals who lack good communication skills, good listening skills and who possess little to no compassion for the people in their care.

In the UK, nurses take a more holistic approach to care by considering and attending to patients and their needs in their totality – physical, emotional, social, economic and spiritual. From first-hand experience, I've recognised that patients prefer this approach. In their eyes, how well they are received into care, how well the nurses speak to them, how well their concerns are listened to etc. far outweighs professional knowledge and actual medical treatment. Many recipients of care, as research now shows, elevate the relevance of bedside manner in the total patient experience. This, then, highlights an area of much-needed improvement in Zimbabwe, one that professionals need to address. Holistic care has a far greater impact on health and wellbeing than any one specialised area of care.

Bedside manner – the importance of care, compassion and empathy – was something I learned about at university, and it has been the bedrock of my practice ever since. I hold myself against strict standards on a daily basis – to communicate in the right manner, at the right time, and in the right place, and to *sincerely* care and empathise. Theodore Roosevelt is attributed to have said, *"Nobody cares how much you know until they know how much you care."* And this is completely relevant in nursing. Being able to communicate clearly, listen attentively and convey a message with compassion is vital. Then topping it off with knowledge and expertise gives patients the ultimate package.

While continuing to reflect on the Zimbabwean healthcare system, I pinpointed another failure on their part – the total collapse of systems allowing registrations of practising healthcare staff to be updated. The medical and nursing bodies used to be responsible for ensuring that staff are fit to practice on an ongoing basis, but now there seems to be a notion of, "Once qualified, always qualified," which ought not to be so. I can safely say there are no checks and balances. There is no basic system that ensures healthcare professionals update their registrations regularly, and they are not required to update their knowledge and skills with ongoing mandatory training.

By nursing here in the UK, I have come to admire and appreciate systems, protocols and procedures that hold professionals to account for their practice. Imagine – why would anyone in their right mind continue to use the same techniques used 10, 20, or even 30 years ago? Especially when relevant research reveals there are better ways of doing things in a less invasive, economical and less harmful way for patients? Yet, in Zimbabwe, doctors and nurses continue to use out-of-date techniques and procedures.

I'm not ignoring the differences between England and Zimbabwe. I realise the latter has a lack of finances and state-of-the-art equipment. Yet, I believe that if the Zimbabwean medical bodies were held accountable for doing the best with what they have, they could do more with the little at hand. After all, a journey of a thousand miles starts with just one step in the right direction.

My dream is to join forces with all levels of healthcare professionals here in the UK who are committed to revive and rebuild Zimbabwe's ailing healthcare system. Together, we could devise sound requirements to reform Zimbabwe's healthcare and put it back on to acceptable levels of care. For those of us who are living in diaspora, we have an obligation to our people back home, and we have been privileged to attain the vast knowledge and skills that could go a very long way in rebuilding our nation.

7

I Started Nursing Studies When
I Was 14 Years Old

I was born in what used to be Czechoslovakia, in the very heart of Europe, and I grew up under the communist regime. In 1991, when I was 12, Czechoslovakia was divided into two states: the Czech Republic and Slovakia. My hometown became part of Slovakia.

The work of the healthcare staff was very much respected during my childhood, but it was recognised that not many girls could study to be nurses. Following the Velvet Revolution in 1989, in which communism fell, everything changed. I started studying at the nursing college in 1993 when I was 14 years old. In Slovakia, it is prescribed by law that everyone has to graduate from school at either 14 or 15 (depending on their date of birth), and then after graduation, they must decide what they wish to study further.

Why did I decide to be a nurse? Well, my elder sister worked as a nurse at the high dependency unit of the University Hospital in Bratislava, Slovakia's capital city. Two of my aunts worked as healthcare assistants in the intensive care unit at the University Hospital in Trenčín, Slovakia. My cousin worked as a nurse in Austria. As a child, I wanted to be a teacher or a nurse so that I could help people, but somehow, it was natural for me to decide on nursing. I think it runs in my family.

Getting into nursing college was very difficult at the time. Prospective students had to sit entrance exams in biology and the Slovak language. A lot of youngsters taking these exams for the second or third time. Out of three hundred students, only sixty candidates were accepted (I was ranked number thirty-one).

In September 1993, I started a 4-year nursing course. My class consisted of thirty-one girls and one boy. For the first year, we only studied theory, which covered many subjects, such as nursing, Slovak language and literature, German language, surgery, general practice, paediatrics, gynaecology, physics, chemistry, mathematics and psychology. It was extremely challenging.

In the second year, after six months, the course included two days per week of practical hospital experience. So, on Thursdays and Fridays from 8:00am until 1:00pm, we worked as student nurses and then returned to the college for three hours of study. The practice at the hospital was very different from the practice of nursing students in the United Kingdom, as I later discovered. In groups of eight, we worked in different departments, and we were supervised and taught by a practical mentor. Each department had its own practical mentor.

The third year continued in the same manner. Additional classes were added, and at the end of the year, we worked in the hospital as students for a whole month.

The fourth year was the most difficult of all. By the end of the year, we had spent time in all of the hospital departments, including neonatal, paediatrics, gynaecology, ITU, surgical, internal medicine, HDU, outpatients, and care of elderly. Then, at the end of our studies in May, we took written and oral exams, and we also had practical exams at the hospital.

After successful completion of my studies at age 18, I wanted to continue studying at university to gain a degree. However, there were two problems: location and money. The hospital university was in another town, and my parents did not have the money for my studies, neither were any scholarships available.

So, I took a job at a nursing home where I worked for eight months. I found the work to be very boring but physically demanding. I worked 12 hours a day, from 6:00am to 6:00pm. Every morning, each of the 22 residents had to shower and be ready for breakfast at 8:30am. Day shifts were covered by two nurses and one healthcare assistant, while the night shift was covered by only one nurse. If that nurse needed help, she could call the on-call nurse, but that only happened on rare occasions. Most of the time, she would have to change the patients' positions and change their diapers all by herself. Half of the residents only required residential care and the other half needed nursing care.

As a qualified nurse, I wanted more experience, so I applied for a place at the hospital. They offered me the choice of working on the cardiology care unit (CCU) or on the intensive care unit (ICU). I chose ICU.

The first few months were so tough that I didn't think I could ever do the job. As a 19-year-old girl, it was a big challenge to adapt to being in a large team of new co-workers and to also become familiar with the various different machines and the medicines I had not heard of before. For the first month, I worked 8-hour shifts from Monday to Friday, but after that, I was assigned to on-call shifts, which was better mentally. I was placed into a team of nurses, and they were all very kind and helpful.

The system of work in this department consisted of eight-hour shifts. There were four groups of nurses who worked together for a few months, after which the teams were rearranged so that we worked with a different mix of people. Each group had eight nurses, one of whom was in charge. As a new nurse, I was allocated the most critically ill patients so that I could learn quickly, but always with support from senior nurses.

The intensive care unit had ten beds, but the most patients we ever had was eight. When necessary, our patients were sent to specialised centres in other cities.

By the end of my first year, I started working in the anaesthesia section because it was a part of the ITU. Twice a year, for a month, we took it in turns to work in anaesthesia from 7:00am to 3:30pm to assist the surgeons with theatre operations. If there was an acute case that needed an emergency operation outside of these hours, one of the nurses would assist.

We also worked as outreach nurses. Whenever there was a cardiac arrest in any department in the hospital, we were called to help.

The hospital didn't have an accident and emergency department, so patients were brought to us directly from the ambulances. In our department, we had an admission area and two rooms where patients were stabilised, if necessary, before being transferred to the theatre, a different hospital, or to the ICU ward. When the nurse in charge took the call from the paramedics, she would appoint a nurse from the group to admit the patient. The appointed nurse then needed to hand over her other patients to a colleague, meaning that a single nurse ended up looking after 2 or 3 critically ill patients at the same time. This is an example of how things could change very quickly, and it made every shift unpredictable. I believe that only a strong person who loves their work can sustain this system whereby the job at hand changed at a moment's notice. Occasionally, I found myself working with two critically ill children at the same time who were both intubated, ventilated and sedated.

After a few years, I decided to leave that hospital because I wanted to work as a nurse in another country.

I had studied German at secondary school, so I looked for work in German-speaking areas. Initially, I tried to find work in Switzerland. Several times, I travelled there for interviews, which cost me a lot of time and money. As the Swiss have a very strict selection process, the interviews consisted of a practical part and an oral interview. During the former, nurses worked for several hours on the hospital ward in which they had applied to work. The point was to determine whether we were suitable to work in the hospital and that specific department. The oral interview covered my knowledge of the German language and the details of my previous work experience. I was finally offered a job at a Swiss hospital, but I was unable to get a work visa.

Subsequently, I got a job as a practice nurse in an Austrian medical centre. The work wasn't very hard. The role involved assisting the doctor, taking blood samples and changing dressings. After three years, I desired to return to a hospital setting, but at that point, if I wanted to stay in Austria, I would have had to complete an Austrian university degree. This would require me studying for two years in Vienna, and the course had a 2-year waiting list. So, I decided that I would go to England to learn English and then return to Austria to study.

Just before Christmas in 2004, I relocated to a city in South West England. During that year, Slovakia joined the European Union, so it was very easy for me to get a job when I arrived. I registered with a nursing agency, and I got a job as a healthcare assistant in a nearby nursing home.

To work as a nurse, I needed to apply for a PIN number, which would take 9-12 months, and since my plan was to return to Austria, I didn't bother at first. However, after several months, I met the man who later became my husband, and so I decided to stay in England. In mid-2005, I applied for a PIN number with the Nursing and Midwifery Council and received it nine months later, in March 2006.

I was excited to get back into nursing, but it was not easy. Since I had no experience of working in an English hospital, I was only offered a job as a locum nurse on the hospital's staff bank. The wards, though, did not need nurses from the bank for they had enough nurses already. Subsequently, I was asked to work as a healthcare assistant on the staff bank instead.

Working as a healthcare assistant helped me a lot. Every shift, I worked in a different department – some days on the surgical ward, and others on the medical ward. I was able to learn the role of healthcare assistants as well as what was expected from the nurses. I noticed that healthcare assistants in England have a different role to those in Slovakia. Back home, healthcare assistants do the job that porters do in England. When I worked in Slovakia, I rarely needed to do the work of a healthcare assistant (English porter). It was only necessary when I needed to transfer patients who were undergoing investigations or when I needed to take blood to the lab (Slovakian hospitals don't have pod systems that carry samples from one department to another).

While working at the hospital, I found part-time work in a nursing home. But then I was offered a full-time job as a nurse on the Care of the Elderly ward where I had been working as a bank nurse for a year. I accepted, and for a while, I had two jobs, but it was difficult to coordinate the shifts, so after a few months,

I decided to quit my job at the nursing home and work only at the hospital.

I ended up working at that hospital for ten years in total. Due to a shortage of nurses, I spent several months in both the winter ward and the gastroenterology department during my time at the hospital.

After seven years, I wanted to try something new, so I took a job at a community hospital. However, the job was very simple, and I felt like I was wasting my previous work experience. It was convenient to work there, for they provided childcare for my little daughter, but from a work perspective, I was not progressing. So, after five months, I returned to my previous job, and the nurse in charge suggested a flexible working pattern that would allow me to look after my daughter. When my daughter started school, I no longer required such flexible hours.

By that time, I felt unfulfilled in my work on the Care of the Elderly ward. I wanted to progress in my career, and I had always wanted to go back to the critical care setting. It was the right time, so I decided to try it.

First, I completed a mentoring course so I could teach student nurses, and this fulfilled me. Then, I applied for a position as a critical care nurse and was invited to an interview. I was successful in getting the job, and in September 2019, I started working as a nurse in an intensive care unit. After several months, I can say that the work is very psychologically demanding. After 20 years, I feel like I am starting at the beginning again. A lot of things have changed: medicines, machines, treatment management … everything is new to me. I am still not sure if this work is suitable for me now since I am older and have a family. I hope that after some more time has passed, and I have gained more practical experience, I will feel more confident. Beginnings are always difficult.

I feel very lucky to work as a nurse in England and to have had the opportunities to nurse in other countries. I love my work, and it is fulfilling me. I often think about what I would do if I was not a nurse. Perhaps I would study to become a teacher as I used to dream of as a child, but I cannot imagine myself doing anything else. Nursing is not for everyone. It is a life mission that one needs to do from their heart.

8

What Did I Just Sign Up For?

———————

I was glad to receive my uniform. It certainly confirmed I was a nurse. Well, a student nurse. To me, it did not make much difference. This was my first day on placement.

Backtrack a couple of years. I came to England in 1999, at the time when all my peers were enrolling into universities across England via international applications from Zimbabwe. I was not one of them. Instead, I came to England on a six-month visitor's visa with the intention of applying directly to a university. My hope was that I would eventually study law. That was my passion.

I had deliberately done art subjects at A-Level, which gave me a good overall grade. I finished at the end of 1997 with 10 points, which was quite impressive, but not good enough to get me into my university of choice to study law. I did not, therefore, get a place to study. This shows how high the standards of academic achievements were in Zimbabwe. My only remaining option of higher education was to do an arts degree at a different university. Ultimately, this would have led me to become a teacher in high school, which was not my dream.

That's why my hope lay in relocating to England and studying law at an English university. I was under the impression it would be an easy ride, but I quickly discovered that the international fees would most definitely cost me an arm and a leg! Nursing, however, was a much easier route with a bursary in tow, meaning my financial worries would be eliminated. Despite that opportunity being available to me, I did not consider it. I had higher aspirations.

After working for a year in Zimbabwe, I arrived in England, but life was not satisfactory; I worked long hours, almost seven days a week, to help my sister with bills and money to send home. This depressed me immensely. I also enrolled at an English college to change my visa to a student one, which allowed me to stay longer than the original six months. However, all of my applications to English universities were proving unfruitful, and I felt like I wasn't doing anything productive with my life. So, at the advice of a friend who was studying medicine in Wisconsin, I applied for the same course. By then, I had been informed that anything related to health and social care would assure me a lifelong career, and I was told the chances of being accepted into the Wisconsin medical school were high. In my mind, medicine was still a greater goal than nursing. I am proud to say that I obtained a place!

And so, I prepared to vacate England permanently – I never wanted to live in the UK again! Moving to America would most certainly improve my life, or so I thought.

I could not apply for an American visa from England because I held a Zimbabwean passport, so I needed to return home, which I did around springtime in the year 2000. Being home made me feel somewhat inferior to my schoolmates who had graduated by then and were starting decent jobs. I was still waiting to pursue my dream job, which frustrated me to the core. Then, I was denied a visa to America without much reason given. I cried as I had never cried before. My life was going backwards, not forwards.

I had not intended to return to England, but since I had three months left on my visa, I reasoned I had nothing to lose.

Days and weeks went by, then in early 2001, one of my relatives made contact and told me that her university was accepting direct applications on the proviso that applicants could prove they had good grades. I applied directly and was invited to an interview for mental health nursing. The university was quite a distance away, but I was determined to try, no matter where it would take me. Just one week later, I received an acceptance letter. I felt so proud of being a university student, but I really had no clue about mental health.

I got accommodation at the nurses' residence close to the university campus. Life seemed fairer and more interesting. I enjoyed mingling with the other student nurses, and I particularly jelled with two ladies who are still very close friends of mine.

Fast-forward to my first day of placement. There I was with absolutely no clue about mental health, allocated to a dementia ward that looked after ladies in the end stages of dementia. Every single one of the patients was aged over 65. I thought, "Oh, my goodness! What have I just signed myself up for?"

The ladies were mostly bedridden or wheelchair-bound; only a few could walk unaided. All of which meant that around 90% needed toileting and feeding. Woah! This was not the nursing I wanted to do! I wanted to be on a ward, yes, and in my uniform, yes, but not toileting, feeding and changing ladies who couldn't communicate much.

But I had to get used to it because it was a three-month placement. My mentor was a stern and rigid lady who was totally obsessed with Robbie Williams. In hindsight, she probably had my best interests at heart, but at the time, I didn't see it that way. In fact, I was petrified of her! She definitely reminded me of my O-Level Geography teacher who scared the living daylights out of all of us in that class. My mentor would ask me about psychosis, delusion, paranoia, schizophrenia, etc., but it was all Greek to me! However, I was determined to prove to her that I really was not daft as I felt she viewed me. And in all honesty, she taught me a lot. I had previously known nothing about mental health, except that mad people in Zimbabwe would carry big sacks on their backs and roam the streets shouting at passers-by in torn clothes. This was not it. I soon started grasping the concept of mental health, and surprisingly, I enjoyed learning about it and nursing those affected.

My course included other placements and a bit of community nursing. I sailed through, learning and adjusting as I went along. I did fairly well in my assignments and managed to pass the 3-year course, after which I registered with the NMC (Nursing and Midwifery Council).

Now, I needed a job, so I applied for various positions and landed my first nursing post in another city, which meant I was on the move again. I worked as a D Grade nurse, as they used to call the newly registered nurses ('D Grade' is the equivalent of what is now termed 'Band 5'). The hospital applied for a work permit on my behalf, and I was granted a 5-year permit.

I quickly realised that nursing as a registered nurse is completely different from nursing as a student or healthcare assistant. I found myself with the responsibility of looking after a 16-bed unit with both males and females in an acute state of mental illness, which meant we were nursing volatile, sometimes unpredictable, individuals. It was good, though, because I learned to think on my feet.

At first, I did not like restraining patients. It scared me. But I soon learned that, sometimes, the only way to contain an individual and make the environment safe was to restrain. And, of course, I was taught the proper techniques to use.

Another thing that became obvious almost immediately was that the skills I acquired at university were not easily applicable in practice. For example, we were taught about 'Unconditional Positive Regard' – it became our nursing mantra. It meant that we needed to accept and support patients regardless of anything they might say or do. That was easier said than done! It was easy to talk about it at university, but it was a different ballgame when patients lashed out physically. Nursing requires patience, I tell you. I had to learn patience, and not only that but empathy, too. Above all, I learned self-restraint and self-awareness in keeping my professional cap on regardless of any situations that came my way. To me, nursing is an enjoyable career, yet it is challenging, both mentally and physically.

One thing I have learned in my career is to acknowledge that nurses are very good at looking after their patients but totally useless at looking after themselves and their colleagues. Nursing wards are full of the most volatile, unpredictable and judgemental human beings, and I am not talking about the patients, but the staff! In my nursing career, I have encountered bullying, harassment and discrimination from patients, but the worst offenders have been the staff I worked alongside. I guess there is a lot of unconscious bias that impacts and clouds some nurses' conduct. I realised that being foreign would mean struggles in regards to professional development, but I also discovered that being a nurse with protected characteristics made me a target for all sorts of mistreatment.

I have, however, learnt to fight ... with hard work, perseverance and kindness. When that fight is acknowledged, life seems less stressful, opportunities arise, and positive relationships emerge.

I have been a nurse for fifteen years now. Do I regret this career choice? Absolutely not! I have learned basic human qualities that are needed to support those who might be at their worst depths of despair. Nursing not only improved my quality of life in terms of attaining property, cars, holidays, etc., but it also improved me as a person.

Through nursing, I have learned to be the advocate for those who do not have a voice; I have learned to be a shoulder for someone to cry on; I have learned to be the ear that listens; I have had to adjust and acknowledge my prejudice against people I feel unfamiliar with or those I put in categories such as the LGBT or Moslem; I have had to embrace the person before the label; I have had to re-adjust my whole thinking in order to develop the skills that ultimately support effective care.

I love my career. I can't judge. I no longer know how to, especially having worked with individuals who had committed heinous crimes due to ill health. I have come a long way. I am a nurse *and* a human, after all.

9

Is Nursing Really Worth It?

"Nursing is not for me!" I cried almost pleadingly to my mother when I was 16. I was about to finish high school and needed to choose my vocation. My father had an ultimatum: "Get a nursing degree, or I will stop supporting your education."

In retrospect, I believe that three key moments led me to where I am today – maybe by a higher force, maybe by destiny, or maybe just by sheer luck – instances whereby I had to make a choice. The choices seemed inconsequential at that time, thoughtless even. Little did I know that they were the pivotal moments that shaped my future. Choosing my course at university was the first. And I did not even have a choice on the matter.

The Philippines is overpopulated. Manpower comes very cheaply, as there is a surplus. So, one must finish their education up to a minimum of a college degree for a chance to get decent-paying employment. The cost of education is pretty high as it is, and in 2006, nursing was one of the most expensive courses to take due to its popularity. Everyone's goal was to go abroad and earn dollars, and nursing offered that golden ticket.

In my country, there is a strong patriarchal structure in the family dynamic. The father is the head, the leader and the decision-maker. My father is a local businessman, and he toiled tirelessly to provide for his wife and six children. He would go away on long trips, explore new ways to earn and start new ventures, just to be able to send his children to university. He believed that education was a person's legacy, that if everything else was taken away from them, their education would remain until the grave. Growing up, my mother, siblings and I relied mostly on his income to make ends meet. We had everything we needed, but there was always the want for more.

There is also an expectation in Filipino families that children who finish school and get a job then give back to support the family. Otherwise, the child is viewed as ungrateful and selfish. Since there were six of us in our family, the goal for all of us was to take the route with the most lucrative outcome – regardless of the child's hopes and dreams – and to finish without delay. The sooner we finished, the sooner we'd get a job, and then the sooner we could help out.

At the time of economic instability, where people had lost their hope in the country, mostly due to the government's corruption, there was (and maybe still is) a mass exodus of the workforce to first world countries. Sadly, a lot of Filipinos even resorted to looking for a "white" boyfriend/girlfriend in the "States" just so they could have a chance to emigrate. So, forcing me to take up nursing was my father's way of ensuring that I had a secure future.

As the youngest, I was always the spoiled one. But there was an unsaid expectation for me to follow at my older siblings' footsteps. Needless to say, my family valued education so much that everyone excelled. I was used to having things decided for me. And in every situation that I was put in, I had to give my best – just like "kuya" (big brother) or "ate" (big sister). I decided to put on a brave face and obediently pursue nursing. I mean, how bad could it be? To my surprise, I loved it! I quickly realised that nursing is a very practical profession – applicable not only to the clinical setting but to everyday life.

In 2010, I graduated with a Bachelor of Science in Nursing degree. In the same year, I passed my licensure exam and finally earned my status as a professional. My parents could not have been prouder. All of their children were now professionals! However, nurses were so abundant that getting a job proved harder than expected. Most graduates resorted to volunteering in hospitals just to gain experience. After relentlessly studying for four years (with summer classes) and paying for tuition fees, accommodation, uniforms, books, and not to mention passing the licensure exam – I wondered whether it was worth it. I could not blame the multitudes of my fellow countrymen for leaving in search of greener pastures.

Asking for financial support from my parents was not an option. My father was nearing retirement age. I needed to pull my weight and start contributing. When my older siblings graduated and started working, they helped my father send the rest of us to school. And now, in gratitude, it was my duty to help. It was time for me to spread my wings and fly. Unfortunately, my flight was low, as the process of going overseas was lengthy and expensive, and nursing in my own country would barely pay for rent. I was stuck in a rut. Even now, it does not make sense to me why the cost of living and goods are extremely high while the pay for professional workers is below minimum wage.

In a stroke of luck, there was a massive boom in the call centre industry at that time. As long as one could speak and write English (pretty much everybody in my country can), they could earn decently. And guess what? A college degree was not required! "Why, oh, why did this just come now?" I thought. "What was the use of me gaining a degree for nursing?"

The call centre was awesome for an inexperienced 21-year-old wide-eyed dreamer. I thought I had found my way out. But after three years in this line of work, I hit the second pivotal moment of my life. I was faced with a fork on the road where one path would keep me in my comfort zone, and the other would lead to unknown possibilities. I realised that to continue where I was would be a dead-end for me. I was just going through the motions of waiting for my pay cheque each month. It was then that I appreciated how I missed being a nurse, and I realised that it was my true calling. I couldn't believe it! I made the decision to take the leap of faith.

Going back to my formative days, I can still remember getting lost in the magical world of Harry Potter, falling in love with Jane Austen's romances, and edging up with Sherlock Holmes' mysteries. So, it is no surprise that I had always dreamed of going to the UK.

At 25, I quit my call-centre job and went back to my first love with a renewed passion. The below minimum wage and 40-hours workweek did not bother me. I stumbled upon the online freelance industry, and somehow, I figured out a way to also work at home as a virtual assistant to an author and businessman in Canada. And since he was paying me in dollars, my additional 20-hour workweek with him earned me the same wage as working full-time in the call centre! But it wasn't easy. For two years, doing both jobs meant that I worked 60 hours a week.

However, I was on a roll! There was a spring in my steps, and I felt unstoppable. But I did not know the specifics just yet.

Six months in, I started making enquiries to different agencies about the requirements for nursing in the UK. They informed me that there would be three major exams but that I only needed to concentrate on the first – which was the formidable IELTS (International English Language Testing System). Only after passing that would the agency look for an employer in the UK and book me for an interview.

So, I paid for a six-month training course for the four IELTS skills: reading, listening, writing and speaking. For all skills, the highest score is 8, and the UK requires 7 in each. And when I failed my first attempt because my writing score was 6.5, I was deflated.

I was back to square one. I had to save up money again for the re-take, as well as spend months retraining while tending my wounded ego. I met a lot of friends through training, though. Some of them were planning to go to the US, others to Canada, and some to Australia or New Zealand. It made me sad to be faced with that fact that all of those intelligent and hard-working professionals were fighting for an escape route and hoping that the exit would lead to a land flowing with milk and honey. One lady, about my age, had just booked her third attempt. I couldn't help but think that it was such a waste of money. I began to doubt myself and wondered if it was all worth it. But I decided to give it one more chance. "If it's not for me, then it's not for me," I reasoned.

Lo and behold, I passed! Then came the third crucial moment in my life – choosing an agency. I did not know how the agency system worked, so I had no idea that the agency I chose would directly influence the area of the UK I would end up in. However, I did not even get to choose an agency! By this point, I was confident enough to tell my cousin, who was already in the UK, that my plan of going to the UK was in motion. So really, it was a case of my cousin knowing a lady who ran an agency in the UK. She instructed me to email all of my credentials to that lady. That lady, who turned out to be lovely, then instructed me to get in touch with their affiliated agency in Manila. Again, I followed blindly and did what was asked.

On a very hot Wednesday afternoon in October 2015, I had a Skype interview with a hospital in Surrey, which I passed with flying colours! From then on, things sped up. I passed my CBT (computer-based test) in November. And in March 2016, I was sitting at the boarding area of Ninoy Aquino International Airport for my flight to London Gatwick. It was then that I met, for the first time, two of my soon-to-be colleagues who have now become, not only my best friends but also family.

When we touched down, we were greeted with the frost of late winter. But that was OK because we were ecstatic to finally be in England! We started working as Band 3 nurses while training for the third and final hurdle – the OSCE (objective structured clinical examination). We were given free accommodation for one month, so we had to look for a more permanent situation while working shifts and studying. Thankfully, the Filipino nurses at the hospital who had been in the UK for longer aided us in our transition, which made things bearable. By April, we found a house to rent. And by July, we all passed the OSCE and finally became Band 5 nurses!

I started in a medical ward, where I unexpectedly met my true love (different story). I have to admit that the healthcare system is totally different from ours back home. Aside from nursing procedures, such as patient assessment, carrying doctors' orders, administering medications etc., it was a huge surprise for me that we also have to do patient washes, mouth care, feeding and rehabilitation. Back home, nurses rarely have to do these things because family members are always there to work with them in accomplishing these things. While a big adjustment, I soon started to appreciate the NHS nursing care and its holistic approach.

All in all, the British people are very nice and polite. One major thing I had to learn was how to be assertive – to speak up, to ask for help when I needed it or to get attention about an urgent matter, even when it caused inconvenience. Assertiveness is not always thought to be a good thing in my culture, so it took a long time for me to realise that saying "no" is not always a bad thing and that it's OK to say "no" without an explanation.

Unfortunately, I experienced a form of bullying and racial discrimination on that ward. It was not only me but also my other international colleagues. The good thing is that we became closer and established real friendships because we went through it together. The hospital later acknowledged the problem and took action. Since then, there have been really productive changes, and I am very happy about it.

Even when I was a student nurse, I always dreamed of being an ICU nurse. I am fascinated with the fact that medicine, modern technology and human skills can bring a person back from the brink of death. After a year on the medical ward, an opportunity arose in ICU. I applied and got the job!

I love ICU! I can truly say I have found my niche. I am where I belong. After three years of learning and mastering skills in that 16-bed ICU, I yearned to explore and develop even more. My boyfriend and I searched for a more specialised unit where we hoped to continue growing our careers, and we found it on the other side of the country!

The move was arduous; it took such a strain on our budget, energy and time! We did not know that we could actually do it seeing as we were still fairly new to living in the country. But we had finished our 3-year contract in that beloved hospital, and it was time to stretch again and see where our hopes and dreams took us!

Currently, we are both ICU nurses in a 46-bed unit, which specialises in burns, neuro, renal, and trauma. Everything is fresh and new again. We are quite excited about where our learning and skills will take us. We believe our new city will be the place where we will buy our own house, settle down and start a family. My boyfriend is even considering pushing through with his dream of becoming a doctor. We see only possibilities!

Looking back, I did not know what I was doing when I made the choices for my future, and most of the decisions were made for me. I was naïve and did not have a clear understanding of how the immigration process works. But I pushed through.

Yes, I miss the sunny weather, my favourite foods, even the organised chaos of the streets and markets, and most of all, my family! But four years living in the UK have allowed me to not only work and earn to have enough to support my family back home but also do the things I love, such as travelling, baking and shopping. I now have a new perspective on life and living. I am inspired, and my hopes and dreams are ablaze with boundless possibilities. Take it from someone who went through it – it is worth it!

10

Why Nursing? I Wanted to Travel!

People often ask, "Why Nursing?" Then they often suggest, "Is it your vocation to help people?"

Well, no … I wanted to travel!

And I also wanted a job that was interesting with little monotony … so, travel and variety were the reasons I wanted to be a nurse.

I went into nursing later in life, at 25 years of age. Previously, I had studied business and finance for three years and then worked in the retail industry for two years. Towards the end of those two years, my main thought was, "Can I do this for the next 40 years?" I knew I could not, so I left that job. For the next three months, I worked at an activity camp for children and teenagers, where I got chatting to a nurse who was also working there. She told me about the many options open to me within nursing, which made me seriously consider it as a career. By the end of the camp, I had made up my mind, and I applied for a general nursing course.

Twenty-five years later, I am still nursing, having definitely achieved what I wanted: travel and an interesting, varied job with very little monotony.

I trained in the UK. I was one of the last to do the old-style Registered General Nurse training. This gave me plenty of practical experience in all areas and departments, which I wanted and needed since nursing is such a hands-on job, and I had not worked in any similar field before.

Initially, having enjoyed working at the activity camp, I thought I would specialise in paediatrics. But after six weeks as a student nurse on the paediatric ward, and having a young boy vomit all over me after having his tonsils and adenoids out, I decided against it. I also felt as though I couldn't help the young patients too much because each and every child wanted their mother, not a nurse. So, maybe I did want to help people, after all?!

During my training, I spent time on the intensive care unit (ICU) and was completely blown away by the knowledge and skills of the nurses who worked in that department. I knew without a doubt that ICU nursing was what I wanted to do. But in those days, nurses couldn't go straight into ICU after qualifying. They had to spend a minimum of two years working on the wards as a way of amalgamating their knowledge. These days, this has changed, as well as the training itself.

After qualifying, I moved away from the training hospital, as I thought, "If I don't do it now, I never will." At the time, I could only get a three-month contract but knew I was more interested in surgical nursing than medical. I ended up spending three years on surgical wards before moving to ICU. It was another seven years before I thought about nursing abroad for any length of time; although I had intended to travel sooner, I enjoyed my jobs within the NHS.

Within those ten years, I did get involved with a charity and spent three months working in South America. There, I experienced nursing outside of a hospital setting, which was extremely different and definitely eye-opening. It surprised me how institutionalised I had become. Looking back, I learned a lot from the doctors I worked with in South America, especially the necessity of common sense in nursing, whether in or outside of the hospital environment. I found charity work to be a good experience; it helped me to appreciate the small things in life that are often taken for granted, and I enjoyed meeting people from different backgrounds.

The charity itself provided expeditions to various countries for young adults who were looking for a challenge. My role as a nurse involved knowing their health history, ensuring their safety and giving basic first aid. It was also about being there for them individually (many had not been abroad before) as well as trying to get them to work as a team.

I will always remember one young man I met on an expedition who had overcome drug abuse. His parents were drug addicts, so it's not surprising that he himself also became addicted. I met him when he was clean, and I was impressed with his teamwork and leadership skills. He easily outshone other young people who came from very privileged backgrounds and were destined for top universities. He showed so much more maturity in comparison and always thought about the team as a whole and the individuals within it.

The whole experience of working overseas in a different environment highlighted my knowledge deficits. Reflection is something that was not particularly documented back then, but it is compulsory now for our nursing registration, and it's a worthwhile exercise, especially when encountering new experiences.

Ten years after qualifying, due to a change in my personal circumstances, I decided to look for a job overseas. It was time to travel with my qualification, not as a volunteer, but as a paid nurse. I was 37 years old, and I chose to go to Australia – a lot older than many (usually, people go before they are 30). Although I was older, the process was not too difficult. I used the services of an agency to get a job in the hospital that had been recommended to me. Word of mouth is definitely good for that sort of thing! The agency sorted out all my paperwork regarding the visa I needed, which was a great help because it is quite complicated and can be long and tedious.

I sorted out all of my nursing paperwork so that the nursing body in Australia could register me. For nurses who want to travel, I highly recommend keeping *all* of your qualification certificates together. Otherwise, locating them can make the process more time-consuming and complicated. I found that the agency wanted my certificates dating back to my school days, so bear that in mind. Also, keep a record of your vaccinations, even from your childhood, if possible, because you will be asked to provide this information.

Upon arrival in Australia, luckily, I found it to be very similar to nursing in the UK. Many nurses and doctors were also British, which helped, and their healthcare system and nursing approach were comparable. There were, of course, some colloquialisms and mannerisms I needed to get used to, but nothing major.

I had always wanted to visit Australia, and working there was excellent! I quickly realised how laid back the Australians are. For example, families of patients in ICU would often have to travel for hours to see their relatives. A six or seven-hour drive for each visit was common, but it never really fazed them. They all had such a practical approach to life, and it was very refreshing.

There seemed to be more private hospitals in Australia compared to the UK, although I didn't work within the private sector due to my visa restrictions.

After three years in Australia, I decided to return to the UK, this time for family reasons – Australia is a very long way away. Technology these days, however, makes it easier to communicate with everyone, and you don't feel the distance with the more direct connections.

Upon my return, I found the pressures within the NHS more intense. But having travelled and experienced new units and working environments, I felt able to cope with the changing pressures. The NHS pay freeze impacted me, however, so I decided to seek another job abroad to save money for a deposit on a property in the UK. My search took me to Abu Dhabi in the United Arab Emirates. Again, my job was organised through an agency. Thankfully, because I had worked abroad previously, I had collected and kept all my educational and health certificates, which the UAE were very strict about.

The British and Australian healthcare systems are a complete contrast to the UAE. Abu Dhabi's healthcare is 100% private, so the approach to caring is very different. It really does depend on money and insurance. And after working in the public sector in the UK and Australia, it was quite a shock. There was also quite a big cultural difference, which took some getting used to.

Their nursing approach, I felt, was very task orientated and tick-box influenced. The hospitals/clinics are basically profit-making organisations. I often felt treatments were given purely to make money instead of putting the patients' health and well-being first. I found the mentality of Emirati patients and relatives disconcerting. Their arrogance and sense of superiority were astounding at times, especially when they believed they knew better than the doctors and nurses. Additionally, because they paid for their healthcare, they thought they should be treated immediately. Quite often, when a patient buzzed for assistance, if the nurse did not arrive quickly enough, the relatives complained.

Occasionally, patients would unscrew their intravenous drips from the cannula when they needed to go to the bathroom. One lady, in particular, did it several times, and because the nurses told her off, she banned them from looking after her. Unfortunately, when incidents like this happened, the management accepted the behaviour of the patients and/or relatives by not supporting the nurses, which exacerbated the situation and the nurses' frustration.

Maybe the management's mantra was (and is): "Keep the patients happy, keep them in hospital, and keep the money coming in." To a certain extent, a nurse has no choice but to change their own approach to caring and adopt the hospital's way of doing things in order to cope with the system and environment ... and remain sane!

Abu Dhabi was certainly an experience. I got what I wanted from it, and I was more than happy to return to the UK fifteen months later – that might be because I am older, but I know I prefer the UK's approach to healthcare, the working environment and the lifestyle in general.

Overall, I am happy with my nursing career and the opportunities it has afforded me, although I do feel nurses are underpaid for what they have to learn and do. We are, however, very lucky, because we will never be unemployed, and the options for diversification are always there.

11

Proud to Be a Nurse

My tale of nursing in diaspora began in Autumn 2000, six months after I had entered the United Kingdom as a visitor from Zimbabwe.

I had previously completed my A-Levels and was waiting to commence my studies in travel and tourism when there was a sudden change to all my plans. My parents could see that, with the way things were going in Zimbabwe, there was no hope for a secure future. Hence, they decided to send us, their kids, to explore, study and secure better futures for ourselves outside of Zimbabwe.

Nonetheless, it was a much-welcomed move. I was willing to lay aside my dreams of travelling the world as a career for something that offered more security. Family friends living abroad advised me that nursing would provide both job security and financial security. It was definitely not a vocation I would have chosen had the circumstances been different, but it was the logical choice for my future overseas. So, while still in Zimbabwe, I made applications to study nursing in the UK, but I was not successful in securing a place with any university. I remember praying and asking God to forgive me for frowning upon nursing and labelling it "a dirty job".

During my 6-month visit, I made a new application to study nursing through UCAS (Universities and Colleges Admissions Services) and was invited for an interview at one university. Within two days, I received a response that said I had been given a conditional offer to study a diploma in higher education nursing. I was thrilled with the offer and spent the remaining time preparing to commence my studies. I took the IELTS test (International English Language Testing System) and passed. Then, in October 2000, I officially became a student nurse!

I was proud of my new role, and I experienced a mixture of excitement and nervousness about what lay ahead. When classes started, I saw there were several other migrants on the course. I felt comforted and soon established friendships. For some reason, the migrants hung around together in smaller groups and occasionally collectively. I had a lot to learn about the first world, the British culture and the cultures of other migrants.

The first shock was calling our tutors by their first names. This was taboo in Zimbabwe, especially when the person was older than you! All professionals were addressed either by their professional title followed by their surname or as Mr/Mrs/Miss so and so. Other migrants and myself found ourselves calling the tutors "Sir" or "Ma'am". But it made them feel uncomfortable, so we acknowledged that we would have to accept the differences in culture and adapt.

The university's international department team helped me to apply for a student visa, and within a short period, my visa was granted. It meant that I could study and also receive a bursary for the duration of my training. I was so grateful!

About four weeks after our training commenced, we were sent to our first placements. My placement was at a respite care unit for adults with learning difficulties. I felt glad that I had been "eased" into the training, for there was a fear deep inside of me that I hadn't opened up to anyone about: I was petrified of general hospitals.

During the first year of training, we were required to do eight weeks of placement in all four fields (adult nursing, children's nursing, learning disability nursing and mental health nursing). So, inevitably, the day I was dreading the most would arrive at some point. I honestly couldn't imagine walking into a general hospital, never mind doing anything else there, and walking out alive. Just the thought of hospitals made me feel numb. I anticipated that the smell of antiseptic would hit my nostrils – the same smell that had assaulted me whenever I walked into the Zimbabwean hospital during the time my mother was ill – and I thought I would pass out or actually die if I smelt it again. I had been deeply scarred by the hospitalisation and subsequent death of my mother in 1996. I struggled with grief and had not stepped foot inside a hospital since then. I just knew that doing so would bring back all the painful memories.

For a few weeks prior to the general nursing placement (my third placement of the year), I couldn't sleep or eat well. To be honest, I think I was more worried about the first day than anything else. I wasn't sure how I was going to cope. I didn't know if I would even be able to walk through the doors or if I would pass out when I did. The one thing I knew, though, was that if I made it in and out of the hospital that day, I would have certainly conquered my fears.

The night before the first day of that placement, I lay awake, tossing and turning in bed. In the morning, I arrived at the hospital half an hour early and walked in with a couple of other students who then pointed me in the direction of the urological ward where my placement would be. I couldn't believe it when I stepped into the building just like that! There was no smell of the dreaded antiseptic. And my thoughts were in order, not racing or spinning like I had imagined they would be. Unbelievably, I had managed to stay calm. It was a big relief, and as I continued walking towards the urological ward, I just knew I could face whatever was coming.

The ward sister was already in and was expecting me. She welcomed me and showed me to the staff room where I could leave my coat and bag. I then made a cup of tea and went to the nurses' station to prepare and wait for the handover. The ward sister was a wonderful person, and she made the whole experience less stressful for me. She introduced me to the team, and during the handover, she made sure to repeat all the abbreviations and tell me what they stood for so that I could understand.

I had been assigned a mentor, so we spent time that day planning my learning objectives. This was the first day of my adult nursing placement, and it had gone well, far beyond my expectations. I was so thankful to God. Getting into bed that night, I knew everything was going to be fine.

Incredibly, I enjoyed this placement more than the previous two (learning disabilities and mental health), and I actually wanted to change my field from learning difficulties. I learned so much in those eight weeks, and it made me feel like "a real student nurse". The support I received from the nurses and the healthcare assistants was amazing. They were kind, caring and professional, quite different from what I had encountered in Zimbabwe. In fact, the rude, unkind, unempathetic nurses back home were the reason I had never, ever considered a nursing career. Thankfully, life took me in that direction anyway, and the UK nurses made me want to be a good nurse.

In my mentor's absence, another nurse, Ghanaian by origin, mentored me. She was much tougher on me and would often say, "You have to work much harder than the locals because of your skin colour. You must prove your worth." At first, I wondered what she meant by that. I thought, "England is a first world country. They don't judge anyone by their skin colour." It wasn't until I qualified as a nurse that her words became a reality.

The remaining two years of training flew by due to the busyness of the course and also trying to work part-time to supplement my income. I didn't experience any abusive treatment, but I heard about some of the other student nurses' complaints.

I completed my course in 2003 and was offered a job in a care home working with adults with learning disabilities and severe challenging behaviour. I had previously only ever dealt with mildly challenging behaviour, so this was a big step for me. I did a lot of reading and shadowing other staff (nurses and support workers) before completing my induction. The care home management then processed a 5-year work visa for me.

One day, one of the residents suddenly started running headlong towards a wall. She then repeatedly banged her head and face into the wall before throwing herself onto the floor and continuing to bang her head. I was shaken to the core, as I had never witnessed anything like it. The emergency alarm was raised, but since the resident was on the floor, staff were unable to restrain her. The only thing they could do was push cushions towards her while remaining at arm's length. They hoped that the cushions would reduce the impact of the banging. The lady, however, threw them away so that she could continue harming herself. Her behaviour continued until she was tired out. Only then did she calm down.

By the time it was all over, I was shaking so badly that I couldn't even stand. I sat in the lounge area, and a colleague made me a cup of tea to try and help me relax. It took about thirty to forty-five minutes for me to calm down. We had a debriefing meeting, but it did nothing for my anxiety. I went to bed that night thinking, "What have I got myself into? What's going to happen when I'm in charge and she kicks off like that? I can't deal with this. I'd better leave now before it's too late." Then I thought, "If I leave, where will I work? How do I know it's going to be better than here? What if it's worse? I'd better stay and see how I get on." And that's how I ended up staying. I remained with that care home for eight years, then returned again for another four years on an "as-required" basis.

From the start, my manager was very supportive of me, but I faced challenges from two nurses, Jane and Louise, who were white English. Jane was a senior nurse, quite knowledgeable, but she seemed to look down upon foreign nurses. She would pass comments like, "If only they could speak English well," or "They make poor decisions," and sometimes she would point to her skin and say we needed more training. I felt she was a racist. Although she tried to be subtle, anyone could tell where her comments were directed.

On top of that, Jane's close friend, Kim, was a support worker at the home, and whenever they were on a shift together, Jane would let Kim make all the decisions. For example, Kim would decide who would work where and with whom, what activities each staff member could do, etc. I found this to be very unprofessional, for it was Jane's responsibility to make these decisions, and she showed favouritism by giving that authority to Kim.

Louise, on the other hand, was an outright bully. I felt her bullying behaviour whenever I had contact with her. Louise's comments and attitude towards me and other foreign nurses intimidated me to the point that I used to shake whenever we were due to work together or whenever I had to hand over to her.

At home, I would worry and stress about meeting or working with Jane or Louise. They crushed my confidence, and after weeks of this abuse and the anxiety it caused, I decided to have a word with my manager.

I remember the day like it was yesterday because she was such a caring and professional woman. When I asked to talk to her, and she realised how unhappy I was, she immediately put a 'Do Not Disturb' sign on the door, unplugged her phone so that it wouldn't interrupt us, and put aside her work to listen to my concerns. She listened to everything and immediately drew up an action plan. She gave me a week of annual leave, then allowed me to come back on night shifts only until a review date, at my request (night shifts meant that I wouldn't be working with Jane or Louise, for they worked day shifts; the only time I would have to see them was for 15-20 minutes during the handover). My manager also booked me onto an assertiveness course.

I'm not quite sure what happened, but two weeks after I returned from leave, Louise was signed off sick with depression. Initially, it was for a month, but then another, and more followed, and she never came back. It's awful to say, but I felt relieved. If it hadn't been *her* signed off with depression, then it would have been *me*. Jane continued working at the care home for about another four months, then decided to leave to travel the world.

I continued working night shifts even after subsequent reviews and supervision. During that time, I developed my clinical and leadership skills to that extent that, after Jane left, I was able to make suggestions and give meaningful input into the care of our residents. For most of that year, I did monthly reviews of all our residents, which gave me a good insight into their needs, the effects of different medications, positive behaviour management strategies, etc. I also gained a lot of knowledge from other staff. I felt better equipped to do my job and soon went back to day shifts, though I never forgot about what I had been through. The job itself was stressful due to the extremely challenging behaviours of the residents, without the added abuse from colleagues. It was a tough environment that required a lot of peer support, and it taught me the importance of teamwork.

There were a few other incidents of abuse in my nursing career, but certainly, none can beat or amount to what I experienced in that first job. Yet, I learned so much from my excellent manager who helped to shape and mould me into a good leader. I cannot thank her enough for her guidance and support. The whole experience developed me positively.

Years later, I'm still working as a nurse. I completed a Master's degree to enhance my practice and am now pursuing a management role. I love my job and enjoy what I do. I can't imagine doing anything else for a living. It's unfortunate that my home country is so economically unstable that the vast majority are living in poverty and that the healthcare system is failing. It used to be my dream to go back home and help develop our healthcare system. The United Kingdom has given me invaluable knowledge, skills and opportunities that I know would be of great benefit to the Zimbabwean healthcare services. However, with the current state of affairs in Zimbabwe, I cannot think of returning there. The help one can offer is limited and most likely to be temporary. So far, the only help I have given is financial contributions towards a new hospital. It's not the level of input I originally had in mind, for I really would like to be part of establishing a service that is accessible to the people who need it the most. However, wherever I practice, I'm still proud to be a nurse.

12

Value for Money?

I originally became interested in nursing, and specifically intensive care nursing, after my close aunt passed away in 2010. I was incredibly impressed with the care she received while in intensive care, and I was also fascinated with the equipment used in caring for critically ill patients. I will always remember the face of the nurse who cared for her, and I'll never forget the time she took to care for my family and me as she was dying.

I also wanted to become a nurse because I love the nurse-patient relationship. In the United States, nursing is really focused on the care given to patients *and* their families. Yes, caring for the patient is the most important, but caring for their family is considered to be equally significant.

And so, in 2016, I began my nursing career after realising that my previous degree in microbiology would not afford me the interaction I desired. In my opinion, sitting in a lab all day was boring! As I already had a bachelor's degree, I was able to do an accelerated 1-year nursing program to obtain a full degree in nursing. There is currently a nursing shortage in the US, so universities receive funding to create as many nurses as possible, obviously to those who qualify.

The following year, when I had completed my nursing program, I knew I wanted to go directly into intensive care. I was fortunate to have two clinical rotations in an intensive care unit at a community hospital where I got to know my future managers, essentially getting hired before graduating.

Intensive care was everything I imagined it would be. Dealing with difficult cases proved to be my strong suit. I was not built to serve eight patients at once, as one does on a ward, where some patients become neglected by default. In ICU, I could focus on one or two patients, know them head-to-toe, and care for them in a critical manner.

I was very happy with my job, but life was about to change. In February 2018, my partner was offered an overseas job in the UK. He accepted, and in November that year, we both moved to England.

While in the US, I secured a job via a Skype interview with my prospective employer. In that particular NHS Trust, I was the first to be employed in ICU using such means. Getting the job was easy, but the process of obtaining my NMC (Nursing and Midwifery Council) PIN number was horrendous. In agreement, I was to work as a Band 4 assistant practitioner until I passed the exams set forth by the NMC, and then I could work as an ICU nurse. The exams consisted of a written exam and a separate in-person skills exam called OSCE (objective structured clinical examination). The written exam was the equivalent of US exam called NCLEX (National Council Licensure Examination), and the OSCE focused only on adult health, for adult intensive care is my subspecialty.

These exams were the first barrier with the NMC. After that, I could then send a formal application to be registered with a PIN. Luckily, I had started the process in June 2018, well before our move to the UK. Applying to the NMC was absolutely awful. They required all of my schooling documents, proof of my use of the English language, a police/FBI background check, and recommendations from my employer and professors. The NMC took many months to complete the background and application checks, taking right up to the deadline they provided for submitting all my documents. I was then informed that there was one document missing, and that sent my application back into the queue and having to wait the full deadline time, yet again. By that time, we had moved to England, and I had started my job as a Band 4 assistant practitioner. It wasn't until three months later that I got the OK to take my OSCE.

The biggest thing that peeved me was the amount of money the NMC took from me for all these steps. The application was £140, the written exam was £100, the OSCE was £1,000, and the admission to the register was £150. I had the unfortunate circumstance of failing my OSCE and had to re-sit at half the cost, £500. Nevertheless, these fees are too high. Thankfully, I had the money to spend on this, but what about the people trying to come to the UK to start a new life? By having these steep charges, the NMC is weeding out those who simply can't afford to apply. All this cost to start working as a nurse at a pay of £12.50 an hour? It is outrageous. As of today, and after my complaints to the NMC (along with others they probably received), they have lowered the OSCE exam cost to £794.

Working as a nurse in the UK is very different from working as a nurse in the USA, and I am less than impressed with nursing in England. I work in a teaching hospital, so we receive many nursing students. The lack of knowledge these students possess regarding simple nursing theories has surprised me. For most of them, after asking them questions, I wonder what they are actually learning in their courses. Rumour has it among nurses themselves here that the nursing education in the UK is not the best, and to me, it shows.

Moreover, in the States, the nursing profession is respected by the community and the employer. Both the UK and the US have a nursing shortage, but the States can fund their nurses because of the private healthcare scheme. Their hospital systems are making a ridiculous amount of money, which means they can pay their nurses better. In the United Kingdom, however, NHS funding has decreased dramatically over the years. Because of this, Band 5 nurses (of which I am one) only make a base pay of £12.50 per hour. And so, the debate of universal healthcare versus private insurance is relevant.

I also believe that nurses in England have a bad reputation because of the media coverage of "nurses gone bad" television shows and real-life stories in the news. In the past, there was a lack of an administrative body for nurses in the United Kingdom. After some nurses had been proven to be incompetent, the media took hold of this, and there was an outcry by the public. Why wasn't there an organisation to protect the public from the awful nurses? Therefore, the NMC became the overseeing body for nurses and midwives. The difference between the US board of nursing (the NSCBN – the National Council of State Boards of Nursing) and the NMC is that the NMC protects the general public while the NSCBN protects the nurse.

I do miss nursing in the United States. There, I worked in a community hospital with an 11-bed intensive care unit. It had a more intimate feel because, generally, I worked with the same crew on each shift. Also, we worked with only two doctors – an ED doctor responsible for the emergency department and a hospitalist in charge of the rest of the hospital. Doctors of every other specialty were only a phone call away if we needed them. Because of this, nurses in the US are a lot more independent, and that's what I miss the most. I had to be at the top of my game in regards to assessment skills. As a nurse in intensive care, I did full-body assessments every four hours (listening to heart and lung sounds, pulses, line care, etc.) and analysed telemetry strips. The pharmacists mixed all our medications, and we had respiratory therapists managing everything ventilator related (I did not need to touch the ventilator settings). Medications were stored in a special electronic cupboard, and nurses gained access to patients' medications by scanning their own fingerprints.

Here, in England, I work at one of the biggest neuro and trauma centres in the country. Working in an ICU with 46 beds, I have 200 other co-workers. After a year, I'm still meeting new people! It's nice to work with multiple doctors, and these doctors do so much more than the doctors in the States. For example, I do not have to put in cannulas, and there is a doctor available whenever needed. In England, us nurses mix all the medications. When discussing this with fellow nurses, they were shocked to learn that nurses in the States do not mix their own medications, their first question being, "Who is responsible for wrong mixing or wrong administration of medications, then?" In England, nurses are the last barrier for the safe administration of medicines, which is why it's essential that we double-check them and properly scan them into the electronic medication administration record. I did feel a little behind, respiratory wise, because I did not have to touch the ventilators in the States. I only knew how to give an oxygen bolus in the case of a patient desaturating. However, this has meant that I have gained new knowledge and skills.

I am happy that I am experiencing nursing in a different country, but I am also excited about returning to nursing in the States when my partner's 3-year contract is over. It is my plan and hope to become a nurse practitioner that specialises in HIV/AIDs. As a gay man, I want to give back to my community and others in different socioeconomic communities by helping eliminate this awful virus and disease. My plan is to do a part-time Doctor of Nursing Practice (DNP) degree while working as a bank nurse or part-time as an ICU nurse to support my way through this higher degree.

Personally, I would not recommend people outside of England migrating here to work as a nurse. Nurses simply are not respected enough in the community, and the pay makes it just not worth it. Since Brexit is looming, we do not know what the value of the GBP will be, but if the value does drop, I will be making less than £12.50 per hour compared to USD. This is simply not enough money. I have two college degrees, and I would be making close to the minimum wage. This is why I have reduced my hours at work from 37.5 to 30 hours per week. The stress of work compared to my pay is just not worth it.

13

The Life of an Agency Nurse

How do I do it? Honestly, how? Every shift I fear losing my nursing PIN number and all the experience I've gained over the last 16 years. For what?

Hospitals are persistently short-staffed, but nurses still have to care. We just have to get on with it! We see our colleagues in the impossible situation of maintaining the safety of their patients while caring for other patients they can't even see because they're located in side rooms. Yet, it is embedded in the culture of most hospital wards and units that the staff just have to get on with it and continue to care.

Despite the UK's care quality commissioner saying that patient safety is at risk and employers need to increase staffing levels, nothing seems to change. Staff continue working in such unbearable conditions because they have bills to pay, food to buy etc. For many, it's all they have ever known, despite official complaints, off-the-record moaning, and filling out incident form after incident form. Day in and day out, month after month, and year after year, nothing has changed. Yes, there is a nation-wide chronic nursing shortage, and many

NHS Trusts are recruiting from abroad, but one can wonder if this recruitment route will be sustainable long-term.

How does a nurse provide the holistic care a patient needs when they have no time to care? At times, I worry about taking a break, only to realise at the end of my shift that I have only been to the toilet once, having drunk hardly any water that day (or night). Shifts leave me physically, emotionally and psychologically exhausted as well as leaving me with aching feet and a hungry tummy. And I have a family to look after when I get home after my twelve-hour shift!

Yes, there is a drive for safer staffing that includes improved patient-to-nurse ratio. In some countries, such as the USA, the Middle East and Australia, the lower patient-to-nurse ratio has proven to improve patients' outcome, with a significant drop in mortality rates. Conversely, the higher the ratio, the lower the quality of care and positive outcomes, and the higher the mortality rates.

When I was growing up, I wanted to be a doctor. It seemed to be a better career option, and adults seemed to approve of this choice, but, unfortunately, I did not achieve the grades that would have led me to study medicine. Looking back, I am glad that I ended up becoming a nurse.

An irresistible opportunity to study nursing in the UK came after my A-Levels, and I took it. Nursing school was so much easier than my A-Level studies, so it was plain sailing, academically. However, I found the clinical placements very challenging. At times, I cried, as caring for someone in a life and death situation was something I had not experienced before. I am so grateful for my mentors and the other students who were there for me. Together, we shared experiences, and I felt that I was not alone in this boat. The more I had patient contact, the easier it became. By the end of my training, I was the one holding the hands of new student nurses, showing them the ropes, reassuring them that it would get better with time, and encouraging them that they would become proficient nurses.

Upon qualifying, I got my first job at the hospital where I had completed my general medicine placement. I worked on the short-stay ward, where patients stayed for 3-5 days before being discharged. I loved the job! The best thing about it was the team; we were like a family. I now work elsewhere, but I miss those members of staff, including the managers who cared for each staff member above and beyond my expectations. They bent over backwards to make sure we achieved our goals, and I am forever grateful for their support. They never looked at me as a nurse of colour, rather as a capable nurse, just like everyone else. The patient-to-nurse ratio was 1 to 12 or 13, but it was manageable due to our great teamwork and the fact that the patients were not critically ill.

One day, when I was busy documenting paperwork at the nurses' station, a patient across the ward called out, "Hey you, black nurse, I don't want you to look after me!" I was stunned. The patient was not even in my care. Everyone around me, including his own relatives, were mortified by his outburst. I didn't deserve to be spoken to like that. Still, it reminded me that I was in diaspora and that some people will judge others by the colour of their skin, not necessarily by their competence and capabilities. I just looked at him and kept quiet. The relatives spoke to the patient, and later that day, he apologised. That was the end of that incident.

Sometimes, I still get called the "coloured nurse". And I'm frequently asked, "Where do you come from?" Even if I say

England, I can sense their disbelief until I tell them my roots. I don't think any white or European nurses ever get called the "white nurse"! Neither are they asked questions about their origins, unless, of course, their accents give away the fact that they are not British.

After five years of working on the short-stay ward, I moved to the intensive care unit (ICU) of the same hospital, and I have been specialising in critical care since then. It has been rewarding for me to work in critical care, having only one or two patients to care for, which is even more manageable. Even though ICU does get busy, in most instances, patients are cared for very well. It's certainly a better situation than some wards where the patient-to-nurse ratio is 1:8, 1:14, 1:32 or more. Such ratios make it impossible to provide holistic care! But when there are shortages, nurses can only do their best with the resources available and hope and pray that no complaints will follow.

Sometimes, people wonder why there is a significant rise in the burnout rate of healthcare professionals, especially nurses. Well, I can tell you that it's the stress that comes with the job and the fear of losing one's PIN number. Most nurses, unfortunately, end up unable to cope, eventually making mistakes due to pressure and fatigue, and even receiving complaints from patients whose needs were not met under their care.

After five years, I left my permanent role on the critical care team. I was finding it difficult to cope with working night shifts, as I was not able to sleep during the day. Despite asking the managers for leniency to work more days than nights, they had to be fair to the other members of staff and so could not treat me differently.

So, I joined a few nursing agencies and worked full-time with them for a while. At one point, I returned to permanent nursing while working part-time as an agency nurse, but the salary of the permanent position was over 50% less than what I had been earning as an agency nurse. Plus, it didn't afford me the freedom of choosing when to work and when not to work, so I resigned and re-commenced full-time nursing through agencies.

I thought about career progression and the possibility of senior management roles, and I did apply for several jobs, but nothing came of it. Unfortunately, statistics show that significant biases, such as racism and nepotism, exist when recruiting managers.[2] Ethnic minorities have a very low chance of progressing to higher posts in the NHS. Therefore, the more senior the job, the fewer BAME (Black, Asian and Minority Ethnic) staff. Most NHS Trusts are trying to improve this situation, but unconscious biases still persist today.

I witnessed this first-hand when I made the move to ICU: Some highly experienced BAME staff applied for certain promotions, but each time, the job was given to a white nurse instead, even though s/he did not always have the same experience that the BAME staff possessed.

It is heart-breaking to watch colleagues go through this, especially in this modern age. The people we train and mentor are still the ones getting all the senior management posts, and most BAME staff are still ending up in lower-grade, lower-paying jobs, despite their extensive experience. This inequality has become such that some BAME staff don't even bother trying

---

2   http://www.nationalhealthexecutive.com/Health-Care-News/nhs-must-tackle-systemic-racism-as-report-shows-staff-discrimination-on-the-rise

to apply for the senior roles anymore. They would rather work as agency nurses and earn more than what the senior managers are earning.

Agency nursing has been the right choice for me. Yes, I lost the benefits of a permanent position, an NHS pension and guaranteed sick pay, and I now have to manage last-minute bookings and cancellations. However, I now have a better work-life balance, I can choose when I want to work, and I receive better pay, all of which outweighs the job security of a permanent nursing role. At least, it works for me at this moment in time.

The other side of the coin is that some full-time nurses believe us agency nurses are milking the system, and so, they make sure to give us all the difficult patients and menial jobs. Their attitude is, "You are earning twice as much money as me, so you deserve to work extra hard! Now, get on with it!" But that's the price we pay for the money we earn.

These nurses forget or are ignorant of the fact that I don't feel valued in the NHS as a BAME person. They perhaps don't realise that my salary pays for my private pension and covers all my expenses and sick-pay insurance. They can't envisage a different future for themselves, but one day, they may decide to do agency work to supplement their salaries, and then they will be treated in the same way they have treated others. They forget that I have considerable experience and that, one day, I may want to return to full-time nursing in the NHS. In which case, I will certainly not even consider working on a unit or ward where I am not treated like a competent and highly-experienced nurse with a valid PIN number, like them. They possibly don't know that agency nurses discuss the situations we find ourselves in and encourage or discourage other nurses from booking a shift in those units. Why not treat all nurses the same, rather than looking upon agency nurses as second-class citizens who deserve this type of treatment? It's unfortunate!

In contrast, however, I have worked in some units where I have been treated so well that I forgot I was working as an agency nurse. These places have removed all the barriers between permanent and agency staff, from top management right down to the staff on the ground. For example, I worked in a unit where I was invited to attend any training that happened to be taking place on the day, including staff meetings. Those people mastered the art of caring, not just for their patients but also for their staff. I speak highly of these units and have recommended many to consider working in one of them. Those who have done so have not looked back since. If, in the future, I find myself looking for a permanent role, I know which hospital wards and units I will approach.

I think it's worthwhile for managers to get out of their comfort zones and meet with managers of other NHS Trusts. That way, they can learn from others and change the culture from the top down. Such negative experiences for staff cannot be allowed to perpetuate in the future, for it slowly destroys staff morale and wellbeing.

I'm not sure how the NHS will cope with Brexit and the accompanying rise of European nurses leaving the UK. It's unfortunate to lose such valued and experienced members of staff in an already staff-strapped health service. This will, undoubtedly, force the NHS to recruit even more BAME international nurses.

I don't regret having worked as a nurse in diaspora. I have learned so much, and I have met so many amazing people: Patients, doctors, nursing staff and managers. The colleagues and managers who have respected me are now etched on my heart, for without them, I would not have achieved all that I wanted to achieve so far. I am glad to have had this opportunity, as I have achieved so much more than I could have by staying in my home country.

For those considering to start a career in nursing, I would say, "Why not?" It can be rewarding, and it can be challenging and stressful, but with time, you can build resilience to cope with whatever comes your way. But never forget to take time to care for yourself. If you're not careful, you can easily be depleted, burnt out, stressed and depressed, which can bring other mental or physical health challenges. Take care of yourself first before you care for others; otherwise, you will do a disservice to them.

The great thing about healthcare is the numerous opportunities available. For example, you could work in offices, wards, recovery theatres, admission units, discharge lounges, emergency units, maternity wards, outpatients, community care settings, private sectors, or you could even start a healthcare business. There is no limit. And with nursing, you can migrate to any country in the world and easily get a job. Finally, you can study towards the career of your choice, such as medicine, research, psychology, physiotherapy, chiropody and much more, or even a different field, for nursing has many transferable skills.

Sometimes, I wonder how long I can continue as an agency nurse. Everyone wants to be appreciated and accepted in their place of work, and I am often affected by racism and inequality. I am sure, though, that in the long run, when I have achieved my personal goals, I will pursue other careers where I will not only be appreciated and accepted but also have a greater impact, as I don't see myself working as a nurse for the rest of my life.

14

Have a Little Faith

I moved to England from South Africa in the year 2000 along with my father, mother and older sister. I was 14 at the time.

My father is British, which enabled my sister and myself to gain British citizenship, for which I am thankful. My mother is South African and was naturalised five years after our arrival. She trained as a nurse in South Africa in the late 1970s. I have a few memories of her returning home from night shifts when I was very young, and I was always happy to see her before I left for nursery school. She stopped nursing not long after I started primary school so that she could be around for me and my sister since we didn't have any family nearby to help. Then, about a year before we moved to the UK, she started nursing again at a retirement village. This helped her to get a job in a nursing home within the first year following our move.

Fast forward a few years, and I needed to start making decisions about which subjects to take for my A-Levels. I'd always had an interest in biology, which was further fuelled by a wonderful secondary school teacher. I'd also completed a St John's Ambulance first aid course while in South Africa, so it was fairly clear where my interests lay. I also had a strong desire to join the British Army after university, possibly as a physiotherapist or a nurse. I still didn't know exactly what I wanted to study at university, though, but I made sure to choose biology and chemistry as two of my four A-Levels. These would enable me to get onto most medical/biological university courses.

After attending a few university open days, I applied for several anatomy and physiology courses. Subsequently, I was offered a place on an anatomy course at my local university, which I accepted. As for my military dreams – I had passed the officer selection process and been offered a place to attend the Royal Military Academy Sandhurst. This meant that I could apply for an army bursary for my university course. My plans were set!

This is where my story gets a little more interesting. In order to write honestly, I must include things from the perspective of my Christian faith, for it has heavily influenced my life. After passing my A-Levels, I decided to take a year out from study to work and earn some money before starting university. My mom suggested applying for a job as a care assistant at the nursing home where she worked. It wasn't glamorous work, but it would give me a taster of working with people in a medical setting, so I applied and was accepted. While waiting for my DBS check to be processed, I took a temporary job at a large pensions and investments firm.

At that time, I used to go jogging with friends a couple of evenings a week. On one occasion, on an ill-lit stretch of road, I glanced over my shoulder before jogging across the road. The next thing I knew, I felt a massive force on my body. I clearly remember thinking in that split second, "I've been hit by a car," while at the same time, a voice within me cried out, "Jesus!" and I heard, "Angels!" I must've passed out shortly after the impact, as when I regained consciousness, I found myself lying on the road a few metres in front of a car.

My shocked and panicked friend was talking to the police nearby, explaining what had happened while I was being attended to by two or three nurses who had been walking home from work at a nearby hospital. It turns out that the driver had been driving at around 40mph in a 30mph zone when he hit me. While lying there, waiting for the ambulance to arrive, I thought, "Well, God, You must want me alive for some reason!"

At A&E, I had four staples put in my scalp for a superficial cut. My limbs were also examined to check whether any bones had been broken, but as none were, I was discharged that same night and received no follow-up treatment. For a long time afterwards, I experienced pain in my right lower leg, to the extent that I could not jog or wear flat shoes.

The accident sparked a desire within me to find God and know Him for myself. I had been raised a Christian and was aware of my mom's devotion and prayer life, but God had always felt distant to me. Later that year, I attended a church youth camp, and the theme of the week was 'Dreams'. I started the week with my plans mapped out: anatomy course at university with a probable bursary, then joining the military afterwards. At the end of the week, though, I faced a crossroads: I could continue with my plans or follow my desire to find God.

I chose the latter. If God's plans for me were university and the army, then that was fine. If it wasn't His plans, that was also 100% fine. I committed to pray about each next step, and at that point, God said, "Bible college."

So, the following Monday, I called the university to let them know I wouldn't be attending the course (which was due to start just three weeks later), and instead, I enrolled at a Bible college.

It was a radical change in direction. It was also a huge step of faith and trust in God because the following year, university fees were going to double, which would present a huge cost to me if God led me in that direction.

During my third year of Bible college, I began praying about what I should do next. My desire was to do God's will for my life, but I still had no idea what that was. About four months later, while driving home one night, I heard the word 'nursing', and a deep peace flooded my soul. I knew my next step! Funnily enough, I had always disregarded nursing, as I didn't want people to think that I was just following in my mother's footsteps.

The following day, I started looking into nursing options and found a degree in adult nursing at another nearby university. I applied and was accepted! Only after the application did I discover that the course came with a bursary, so I didn't have any university fees to pay! I was thankful that I wouldn't have any debt and would be able to get a job at the end of it.

I started the course in September 2008 and found it very tough. It was a 3-year course, and six months of each year were spent working full-time as a student nurse in various hospital and community placements for free. In addition to my studies and placements, I worked a 12-hour shift as a care assistant every Saturday to earn some money to cover my transport costs. Although challenging, I stuck at it as I believed God had led me to do the course.

Near the end of my final year, I again asked God to lead me and show me which job to take. I'd received verbal offers from theatre recovery as well as a respiratory ward, both of which I'd enjoyed. The other possibility was to apply for a full-time job at the nursing home where I'd been working part-time. The advice we had all been given from our tutors was to work in a hospital ward to solidify our skills and teaching. After some time, I only felt peace about the nursing home option – the illogical choice. So, I spoke to the manager, and she said that she would love to offer me a job, but there were no nurse vacancies at that time. Her response confused me a bit, as I thought this was what God had led me to do.

A month or so later, a tragedy occurred. One of the nurses at the nursing home, a young male in his 40s, developed a rare and severe infection and passed away within a few days. My manager approached me shortly afterwards and offered me a job. I accepted. Although I don't believe that God caused that tragedy, I do believe He knew that it was going to happen.

Three months after I started working as a qualified nurse at the nursing home, I fell pregnant. My husband and I had only been married for a year, and we had not planned to start a family so soon. I found it difficult to tell my manager, but she was very supportive when I did. She also told me that I would qualify for maternity pay since I had been employed by the company as a care assistant beforehand. I was amazed, for it was not something I could have planned. If I had followed the advice of my tutors and chosen a hospital job, I wouldn't have qualified for maternity pay because the NHS rules state that an employee only qualifies after a year of employment.

I have enjoyed my work at the nursing home. It has been the right option for me in so many ways. The shifts are set on a two-weekly rota, which enables staff to plan ahead and enjoy other commitments. Most hospital wards will have a new rota every month, with a combination of day and night shifts. I think I would have found that very stressful, especially when trying to manage family life, and now I have three young children.

There is such a variety of jobs and settings available to nurses, enabling nurses to find something that fits their priorities. My priority at the moment is family, and so I'm currently doing 'bank' shifts on weekends at the nursing home. Trying to work shifts during the week would mean that I would have to pay for childcare during school holidays. The cost of childcare has recently increased, and for three children, it would cost the same amount per hour as what I could earn!

Another reason the nursing home has turned out to be the right choice is that I have such a supportive manager. During my student years, I was exposed to many different management styles, but my manager at the care home has been inspirational. She has transformed the workplace into a top dementia care facility, and as such, it has received many prestigious awards. She expects high standards but also equips staff to achieve them. For example, the company arranges and pays for all staff training (as well as paying staff for attending training). As a result, staff feel like they are making a difference to those that they care for. My advice to any new nurse would be to find a workplace where the staff and management are supportive of one another. Nursing can be a physically and emotionally draining job, so we need all the support we can get.

Thank you for taking the time to read my story, and I hope that it encourages you to know that you don't have to carry all of the weight on your own shoulders. Sometimes you just need to have a little faith.

15

Hats off to All the Nurses!

I am originally from Zimbabwe and was a qualified high school teacher prior to migrating to the USA.

Initially, I hoped to continue my teaching career in diaspora. But when I contacted some American universities to check whether my diploma would make me eligible to work as a teacher in the US, I was told I would have to re-do my teacher training completely because I was British trained. According to them, the British system is completely different from the American system. This didn't resonate with me. However, when I emigrated, I started re-training since there was no other way for me to be a teacher in America. And when I checked the education and teaching books used in the American university libraries, I found that they contained the same books I had studied during my teacher training in Zimbabwe! After just three months, I concluded that giving up teaching as a profession was better than re-doing it. The road to qualifying was just too long because students have to take prerequisites as well as electives.

That meant I had to choose a new profession that would sustain my family both locally and abroad. I explored many careers, but not nursing. I made attempts to study meteorology or radiology, but neither of these worked out. Eventually, I chose nursing because of its reward as one of the best paying jobs. It wasn't an easy route, though.

Nursing school itself was a challenge for I had to maintain a certain GPA (grade point average) to remain in the program. Initially, I studied towards becoming a licensed practical nurse (LPN), which took two years. After successfully completing the exam, I was able to work as an LPN, which I did for a while to take a break from studying. But, not too long after, I returned to university to gain a nursing degree. Working as an LPN at the same time as studying facilitated a better income for me. My first job as an LPN was at a long-term care facility. I enjoyed it.

My hard work paid off, and two years later, I earned a Bachelor's degree in nursing. At first, I thought it was better to deal 'with the devil I knew', so I stayed within the long-term care facility. This was not the best because the nurse to patient ratio was horrible (1:65). It sounds ridiculous, but that's what it was. I had so much to consider, including my license safety, patient safety, and my personal safety.

The next challenging step was the NCLEX exam (National Council Licensure Examination), which would enable me to work as a registered nurse (RN). About three months later, I took the test. If I had ever prayed, I prayed harder this time for success – and I passed!

Following that, I engaged in a job-hunting spree, which resulted in my working on an oncology unit of an acute care facility hospital.

Even though I have not had an opportunity to work as a nurse in Zimbabwe, I do remember the healthcare set-up, and there are many differences in nursing between the two countries. For starters, in Zimbabwe, many of the nurses are cruel and uncaring – as a patient, I experienced this first-hand. But in the US, nurses will not mistreat patients. They are very respectful and operate within the understanding of patient-nurse respect. It is a fairer system. Don't get me wrong on this one – abuse still happens in America, but it is very minimal because it has adverse effects on one's license to practice as a nurse. Personally, I regularly feel unsettled about the risk of a patient or a member of their family filing a lawsuit against me, for that could mean losing my license. As an element of protection, nurses are advised to obtain malpractice insurance. Overall, though, nurses try to do their best because of the unseen threat of a lawsuit. And it does enhance patient care.

Working conditions and pay is another major difference. In America, we have patient care assistants who work hand in hand with the nurses in providing activities of daily living (ADL). Nurses provide all care, but the care is enhanced with helpers around. This extra help is not available in my country of origin, but it would definitely help in fostering better care. On the salary front, nurses in America are paid considerably more than those back home. The pay is so good that it can hardly compete with any other profession in the US.

A further difference is that nurses back home are empowered across the board and basically run the show. They do everything, except, of course, some of the duties designed for physicians. In the USA, however, nurses have specialty areas, which are solely the individual's choice. I feel this system limits one's capabilities, unless one is prepared to specialize in one area and then move onto the next. But for someone trying to build experience, this is not ideal.

Although I originally became a nurse because of its financial reward, now that I am in the profession, I realize that it's not about the pay. I enjoy taking care of patients, and I love what I do, even though, at times, it can be emotionally challenging. I still work on the same oncology unit, and this means I sometimes care for patients from the time of their diagnosis to the time they die. I go through the grief process with them; we cry together, laugh, joke, and sometimes, we just remain silent. Attachment is inevitable, and that intensifies the challenges of my job. Pay-wise, it is not the best because I am just starting out, but the contentment I feel when my manager passes on a patient's thanks or compliment makes me glad that I am a nurse.

I am happy with my decision to migrate. And it was worth the hassle to train in the US, for I didn't go through any of the frustrations that many foreign nurses encounter when they arrive here, such as meeting all the requirements of the American Nurses Association (ANA).

When I was younger, I never thought I would live and work in diaspora, but if I hadn't left the shores of Africa, I would never have explored the field of nursing. Because teachers are poorly paid in Zimbabwe, I would likely have left teaching anyway and started a business, not realizing the joys of being a healthcare professional. Migration has helped me understand the different types of classes that exist and how one can achieve anything, regardless of their background. I love nursing and hats off to all nurses.

My future looks bright at the moment, and I look forward to advancing my career. I have one final nursing ambition, which is to obtain a doctorate degree in this field. This will enable me to do more than just bedside care, and it may be the route to which I can open my own private practice.

Nursing education in America is hard. It takes sacrifice, determination, humility, patience, and endurance. However, it is very rewarding, and jobs are assured. Once you get your license, the sky is the limit. You can explore any specialty, but always remember that nurses are born, not made.

16

I Am One of the Spaniards

I am one of the Spaniards that migrated to England with the dream of better working rights, a better salary and learning something new every day.

Becoming a nurse was something I had dreamed about since I was little. My twin cousins were poorly once, and a nurse came to my uncle's house to give them some treatment. I was fascinated by this lady – her uniform, shoes, gadgets and first aid kit. She said I was too small to stay in the room, so she ushered me outside. When she later came out of the room, I asked her, "Who are you?" She told me that she was a nurse, and I asked to see her identity card as proof. She smiled and showed me her government photo ID. I was impressed. Soon after, I started questioning my mother about what I needed to do to become a nurse.

Mother said, "If you want to be a nurse, you need to study a lot."

"Ok," I replied, "I will start today!"

And I did. And I still do, because nursing requires continuous development. Nurses are constantly reviewing new protocols, new evidence-based studies, new technologies etc. These things are the reason I am still in this profession; I will never get bored of nursing because there are a variety of departments in which a nurse can work, and there is always a myriad of new things to learn.

As I grew, I became more interested in anatomy, physiology, science and biology. By the time I went to nursing school, there was a lot of competition to become a nurse, but I managed to get a place at university. Following three years of intensive training, I qualified as a nurse in 2005, aged 21.

Soon after, I started working at a nursing home. The residents looked at me with a scared expression on their faces. I bet they had the same feeling I have now when I see people in their 20s, young and inexperienced with a lot of dreams!

A year later, I realised that the job was not for me. I felt I was too young to witness so many diseases and deaths. Plus, I wanted to travel the world. That dream, however, was delayed because I received a job offer that I could not refuse – my dream job in an accident and emergency department! Although it was not a permanent position, my contract was renewed annually, and I ended up spending almost eight years in that department (in Spain, all healthcare positions start on short-term contracts, and it is very difficult to secure a permanent one).

One of the first things I noticed was that a lot of our patients were from the UK. The hospital was located in a popular tourist area, and so, British patients came through our department almost every day. To improve my nursing care, I decided to enrol in a language school and learn English. My father always used to say, "Children! Learn English!" Funnily enough, he could not say a word in English himself, but he had the wisdom to encourage us to learn it. I wished I had taken his advice when I was younger, but as they say, it's never too late, and so, I studied and learned English.

In 2008, an economic crisis hit Spain, one that dragged on for several years. By 2013, the national health service was reducing their staffing levels, and as part of that, my contract at the A&E department was terminated. Over the next few months, I went from one job to another in various different settings. Due to the economic situation, after just a month or two, I was dismissed, only to be recruited elsewhere a few days later. I did not like the precariousness of it all.

Having heard a lot about job opportunities in Australia, America and the United Kingdom, I decided it was the right time to emigrate. And, for numerous reasons, my sights were set on the UK: it was convenient in terms of the flight time and cost; being an EU citizen, the paperwork was easier; and I also wanted to progress in my English-speaking skills. So, I thought, "I'll try it for a year."

I submitted an application with the help of a recruitment agency and was invited to an interview in Madrid. I did not think twice, and I got on a plane. Along with other hopeful nurses, I took some exams and attended a face-to-face interview. Two days after returning home, I received a call with the good news that they liked my skills and experience, that I had passed the interview, and I was then offered a permanent position in England. The word 'permanent' sounded like a dream to me!

Next, I registered with the NMC (Nurses and Midwifery Council) in England, which was easier than I expected. I went to a solicitor to have my documents legally notarized, then I sent the paperwork to an agency that translated everything. A few months later, I was ready to go. I received my nursing PIN number in mid-September 2013, so I booked my flight for 1st October!

My parents were in shock. For the first time in twenty-nine years, I was about to leave home. I reminded my father, "You always said I should learn English, so I am just following your desire!" For sure, he was disappointed.

When I landed in England, it was foggy, wet, raining and dark. I could not see a metre in front of me! However, I was happy. I looked forward to my new adventure, and I relished the nice feeling that good things were coming!

I was employed to work in the emergency department of a local hospital, and I quickly realised that the UK has many different ways of working. After eight years of nursing in Spain, I could not believe that things could be so dissimilar. Some things shocked me, such as the high security, the protocols, the health and safety measures, the double-checking of medication, and the training needed for advanced specialist techniques. And everything had to be evidence-based. Nothing about it compared with working in Spain. There, after qualifying, further training is not mandatory, so nurses generally learn by observing their more experienced colleagues. The hospital I worked in did provide some training at random times on non-specific topics, but even then, it was our responsibility to enrol. Also, nurses in Spain are lucky if they work on a unit with all the protocols up to date!

But not everything was perfect about working in England. Retrospectively, two things happened that still make me feel frustrated. If I could go back, I would make sure they did not happen again.

Firstly, at my interview, I was told that I would be paid according to my experience, but this turned out to be untrue. When I signed the contract, nothing was written clearly about my salary, only about the range of payment at that time, something between £21 – £25k. I thought I would be paid in the highest part of this bracket because I had eight years' experience. After my first payment, I realised this was not the case. I tried to raise a complaint about this, but I could not get it sorted. The people in the HR department made excuses, saying that I had already signed the contract and they could not change it, and so on. I felt as if I would lose my job if I made a fuss about it. Of course, I wanted the job, so I left it at that. But, certainly, I was not a newly qualified nurse, and they took advantage of me.

Secondly, during the induction, HR representatives came to give us some advice, and they insisted on us having an NHS pension, emphasising the importance of it for the future. Now, after five years of living and working in the UK, I am considering returning home, but I cannot claim any of my NHS pension money, and moreover, I cannot transfer it to any Spanish provider because it is not on the QROPS list (Qualifying Recognised Overseas Pension Scheme). So, I need to wait until I retire before I see it. This is just not right and not fair. Since I am a foreigner, they should have made the facts clearer so that I understood the implications of my decision.

Mostly, I felt supported by my colleagues. For sure, some were not very welcoming, but I was grateful to find those who were. In general, patients and relatives referred to me (and others like me) as "the foreigner". They often commented that we were brave to leave our homelands to settle and work in another country – in diaspora – as they could not contemplate doing so themselves. From the start, I got the impression that the British people were very proud of the nurses. Patients gave us a lot of letters, cards and chocolate boxes to show their gratitude for our kindness.

Outside of the hospital, I had a good social life. I always tried to get involved in local activities, nice walks, a few trips inside the country and others a bit further afield, and I also socialised with my workmates. Living in a shared house was a massive change for me, having always lived at home, and I could probably fill an entire book with stories of house-sharing! Sometimes I questioned, "Why did I start this adventure? Why did I want to be on this rollercoaster journey?" There were many highs and many lows.

By far, the worst experience in my nursing career happened in England when I witnessed the death of a newborn baby. It was emotionally devastating.

* * *

Curiosities about my experience of working in the UK are:

- Shifts patterns: These were released every six weeks, more or less, which often made it difficult to organise my personal life. At the A&E department in Spain, the manager released an annual rota, which meant I could easily plan my life around my shifts, even months in advance.
- Unpaid breaks: When I realised our breaks were unpaid, I was speechless. I worked 13-hour shifts but was only paid for 12!
- Reduced hours: There is a system by which nurses can reduce their hours to create a life-work balance. So, I took the opportunity and reduced my hours. Doing just one less shift per week made a big difference! Back home, we cannot do this unless there is a valid reason, such as childcare, studying or caring for elderly relatives.
- Off-sick system: In Spain, if a nurse is sick, they must stay at home until they are fit to work. But in England, I experienced the opposite. I often saw nurses who were 'off sick' working. Granted, they were not in a seriously ill condition that would have posed any risk to patients, but they would return to work and do non-patient contact jobs, such as admin. For instance, I saw a nurse return to work with an injured arm

in a cast and another nurse with eczema on her hands that had not fully healed. To me, it was so weird! Luckily enough, I only got poorly once, and I could not get out of bed, so I couldn't return even if I wanted to.

- Holidays: It was nice to have seven weeks off, but I was not allowed to take them all together. We had to spread them out during the year. In Spain, nurses received only four weeks off, but at least we could take them all in once. We could also request an extra eight days throughout the year.
- Nurses in a dress: When I became a nurse in Spain, the nursing 'dress' was already memorabilia from the olden days, some kind of vintage apparel found in a museum! But in the UK, it is still alive! That was very funny and interesting.
- Supernumerary period: This is a period for nurses to familiarise themselves with their new surroundings. I think it is quite handy to have this process to adapt to a new job. It caused me to relax and gave me the chance to get to know my team, where everything was kept, the procedures, all the login passwords for the computer system and more. I wish we could have this system back home because it would reduce mistakes overall for newly qualified nurses.

My advice to other nurses or those training to be one is: eat healthily, sleep when you can, get involved in activities outside of work, forget about work when your shift is over, then get back into nursing-mode 5 minutes before you start the next shift. It is really important for us nurses to look after ourselves, physically, mentally and emotionally. Being able to switch off is essential to maintaining our overall health and not becoming burnt out because we constantly see the unpleasant parts of life.

After 13 years of being a nurse, I would like to say that I am prouder, I am stronger, I am more knowledgeable and I am happier. Yes, sometimes, it is a challenging career, but it often gives me positive vibes.

I highly recommend the experience of travelling, working and learning a new language, getting out of your comfort zone. You'll discover new ways of working, new ideas and new values. Plus, you'll gain a lot of new friends and learn a lot about yourself. I missed my family, my friends and the weather, but at the same time, I became stronger as a person. Migration is frequently portrayed in the news as a bad thing, and there appears to be a lot of fear about different cultures coming together. But I would not change my decision to migrate, and I can honestly say that it has been an enriching experience.

Now, due to Brexit, my time in the UK is coming to an end, and I am planning to return home. I know it won't be easy at first, and I know it will mean returning to short-term job positions. The future looks quite uncertain, but equally, I feel positive about what is to come.

Even if Brexit was not on the cards, I don't think I could stay in the UK long term. I like England and will always be grateful for the opportunities given to me here, but the older I get, the more I miss my home, my family and the Spanish food and weather. With Brexit looming, it is not only about the racism that the radical right has generated, but it is also about feeling isolated, which shouldn't occur in any country or continent. These are uncertain times for a country that I had idealised as giving opportunities of freedom and equality for the minority.

17

The Burnout Was Palpable

In Zimbabwe, the most prestigious careers were found in engineering, aviation, medicine and law. Although nursing plays a very important role in the career stratosphere of the African society, there is a general misconception that it is on a parallel latitude as teaching, policing or social and civic careers.

When I eventually arrived in the United States, I discovered that the opinion about nursing was quite different. A certain level of pride was evident when people talked about the value of nurses and the obligations they fulfil. In America, I could pursue this career, knowing that I would be contributing to society and making a decent living in a profession that was respected.

The visa office in Zimbabwe took longer than usual to process my student visa, which delayed my departure from my motherland as well as my start at college to complete the required academic prerequisites for admission into a nursing program. And since I arrived late in the academic year, most of the classes in the first semester were already full. Unfortunately for me, this meant that I wasn't able to achieve the course load needed to be considered a full-time student, and that meant my status was automatically 'illegal immigrant'. Urgency and patience were of utmost importance as the next semester would provide the chance to be reinstated as a full-time student, and that would legitimize my immigration status.

On top of that, as a new immigrant, I needed to adjust to a new environment, culture and unfamiliar terrain. There were challenges with how I was perceived (cultural differences), academic responsibilities and punctuality; all these factors imposed extra barriers in transitioning to life in America.

The nursing school had a high population of international and multicultural students, which furthered the financial gains of the institution. However, the personnel did not provide any of us with the fundamental survival tools to navigate the inherent cultural and systemic barriers. The school had an international student advisor who encouraged students into nursing, citing the employment demand as a reason. He also asked students to refer others to the institution, no doubt to keep it full. But there was no guarantee that the new foreign students would be given the support or help they needed to complete the program, nor that they would receive career guidance.

Since my immigration documentation only permitted me to study at that particular institution, I did not have the luxury of transferring to a different one. Otherwise, I would have definitely sought to transfer.

The next semester came around, and the full course load was available to me, but I then had to come to grips with the expensive tuition bill. The expense of American education to a citizen is already unbearable, so as an international student, it was beyond impossible for me to pay my tuition and living expenses. I reached out to family and church members while picking up odd cash-in-hand jobs to safeguard my education.

Speaking of jobs, they became very difficult to secure. At that point, student visas did not make provision for employment, so anyone providing employment to international students with no work permit was doing so illegally. Eventually, a nursing home offered me employment, and even they re-considered due to the student visa/work permit issue. However, for some reason, they went ahead and hired me. I also landed a job in a factory.

And so, my routine became a daily toil of working in the factory by day, attending evening classes at college and working night shifts at the nursing home. This, though, was not sustainable. It came with burn out, a lack of concentration and an inability to keep up with the jobs while maintaining a competitive GPA to get into the actual nursing program.

I spent three years trying to fulfil the academic requirements to be admitted into the nursing program, which, according to the international student adviser, should have taken me, at most, one year. My situation was dire, both financially and academically. It became clear that a critical decision had to be made.

And the tide of life saw me toss my dream to Canada. In Canada, I didn't have any family affiliation, which was a different level of challenge altogether, but within a year, my nursing journey was revived. Upon research, I discovered an indirect pathway of getting onto a nursing four-semester program. It was via an adult learning centre that offered the prerequisite training and a guaranteed place in the second semester of nursing college (this pathway covered the same courses covered in the first semester, which meant that students could go straight into the second). At long last, the dream was re-ignited, and the torch of determination was as bright as ever.

Eight months later, and I had successfully completed the academic prerequisites for nursing college! The adult learning centre automatically registered me at the college, and all I needed to do was to pay the tuition bill. This moment cannot be over-emphasized as life-changing. For the first time, my future was bright, and I could see the light at the end of the tunnel. I had finally achieved my goal of getting into nursing college, which was particularly sweet, considering I had spent three years in the States on a career treadmill. The next three semesters were just a passage of time, though there were challenges ahead.

During that second semester (my first actually at the nursing school), a test of faith emerged during my clinical rotations. It occurred because my mentor held biases and evaluated my performance unfairly, and I did not know how to approach her about it. For the first time, my practical performance in Canada was not to the same standard as my classroom performance, even though I was applying my knowledge to the clinical field, as before. Somehow, though, at my next evaluation, my mentor mentioned that she had not been aware of my good academic merits. After that, all of my evaluations were positive, and I was even appointed to supervise and lead other students. Thankfully, despite the rough period, there was no need for me to repeat any of the courses.

Once graduated, the world of nursing opened its doors with endless potential. I was naïve and full of hope as a new nurse in the workforce. And I looked forward to paying off outstanding loans to banks, friends and family. But I still needed to complete a licensing exam. In the meantime, I gained a temporary license to work while studying for the exam. Under temporary license requirements, one can only work if they have a fully-licensed nurse supervising them, and there were only a handful of employers willing to take on an unlicensed new graduate.

However, employment agencies had access to many healthcare facilities, which made it possible to leapfrog this hindrance.

My first assignment through an agency wasn't a good experience. It was at a nursing home, but the working environment was unhealthy because each nurse was responsible for forty patients. Medication (oral, injection or topical) administration was done within a 2-hour window, and if that was missed, it was considered as a medication error. For forty patients, this meant a maximum of three minutes per patient! This was the norm in most nursing homes, but it goes without saying that it bred a poor quality of care for it was an impossible task. Finding the patient, confirming their identity, administering the right drug *and* documenting it within three minutes required a miracle worker. Some patients needed the pills crushed and mixed with applesauce while some preferred taking one at a time, understandable when they had multiple to take.

Between each 'medicine window', nurses had to squeeze in everything else, such as dealing with family members, dressings, assessments and other staff duties. All in all, it was a herculean task. Either one started the shift way earlier or cut corners to make it through, but then patient care was compromised. No amount of training could prepare anyone to function in that kind of atmosphere. The job required mental alertness, not to mention physical strength. At the end of each shift, moans and groans with soreness were reminiscent of my American experience of working at the factory by day, studying in the evenings and working at the nursing home by night. It wasn't the nursing career I had imagined and worked so hard for.

The agency sent me to different settings, but the job load and challenges were equivalent, sometimes worse. Certainly, it was not a sustainable situation. Some nurses needed to take pain medication just to get through a shift. The burnout was definitely palpable, as sleep became the go-to solution. However, in turn, that made it difficult to keep up with the prep exam schedule. And one could forget about having a social life or looking after their own wellbeing.

Something had to be done. Certification exam dates were available only three times a year, and candidates were allowed just three attempts. This licensing exam was 'do or die'. If I failed even the first attempt, I would lose my temporary license and wouldn't be able to work. And if I failed all three attempts, I would no longer be able to be a nurse in the province. The reality check hit me hard. I cut down work hours and studied more.

Over the next month, long nights and after-shift toiling became my study routine. The grind continued even the night before the exam; I found myself reviewing last-minute details, sleeping late.

The exam itself was eight hours long, divided into two four-hour blocks of two hundred questions each. The first block felt overwhelming, and the questions were very foreign. To make matters worse, during the scheduled break, most students were gloating about how easy they had found the first four hours. This worsened my fear of not passing my licensing exam after sacrificing and enduring seven treacherous years to get to that point. I went into the second half like I was on the way to a firing squad or a death trap! But, lo and behold, the questions were more recognizable. My inner voice shouted, "Hallelujah!"

After eight hours, I didn't know how to feel. I went home and slept for two days straight days with only food and bathroom breaks.

While awaiting my results, I continued with agency work on my temporary license. One day, an incident arose because I was unable to insert a catheter during the usual 'three-minute' patient care. I asked for help, but everyone else already had too much on their hands to assist me (even though I was meant to be supervised, I wasn't). I did not want to leave it for the oncoming nurse, for she already had forty patients to worry about, but I had no choice. Upon finding out about the catheter issue, the oncoming nurse was very upset to the point of expressing her dissatisfaction. She told me how incompetent I was and how it was a routine procedure that anyone could do. There it was: workplace abuse, coming at me through a thin-built, frail nurse frustrated with the system while oblivious to her frustration and misdirected anguish. It was obvious that the stress had overcome her will, patience and desire to care for patients. Just like most nurses who worked themselves to a standstill and/or inevitable dependence on pain medication just to make it through a shift.

This time, I felt it was necessary to take action and get out of the toxic environment. While on my way out, the oncoming nurse was asking for assistance to insert the catheter that I had been unable to do. This was to no avail, and the patient had to be sent to hospital. I walked out of there with my head held high.

Later, I called the agency to cancel my shifts at that particular nursing home. This brought me to the realization that working through an agency gave me the power to choose my working environments, which has to be the single most important luxury. I started choosing safe working environments and avoiding hazardous settings, but I could only enjoy this freedom of choice long-term if I passed my exam, and I was still waiting to hear.

Then the day arrived. Upon getting home from a shift, I saw that I had mail from the licensing board. Back at nursing school, we had often talked about the size of the envelope determining whether one had passed or failed (rumor was that a big envelope meant you failed, while a small envelope meant a pass). With an envelope in hand, my emotions got the better of me. At that point, the size was indifferent, as I couldn't even differentiate the size of the envelope! Trembling and sweating, I opened the envelope. My heart was beating out of my chest as I unfolded the letter. To my delight, I passed!! At last, I had reached my goal, and a sense of calmness settled over me.

However, the nursing board required a separate application for licensure, which I found to be inefficient, for they could have added a checkbox to the exam application that said the board could process the application with the information already provided. Nevertheless, I applied and was fully registered after a couple of weeks.

I started applying for jobs all over the city, and I received lots of call-backs – so many that I couldn't keep up with them all. It was exciting, but at the same time, I had to grapple with the reality that giving up agency work meant surrendering my power to choose my work setting, and I couldn't guarantee that I would end up in a safe place.

As a newly licensed nurse, there were more good days than bad, and I gradually started falling in love with nursing. I found taking care of the elderly to be rewarding, especially with the amount of wisdom and love they impart. On one occasion, as I entered a patient's room, I saw that she was on the phone to her daughter. The old lady looked over the top of her lenses, and a smile spread over her face. To her daughter, she exclaimed, "Goodness, gracious! Guess who is here? It's my nurse. You need to come and see her." And then the phone call came to a sudden end. I could hear the excitement in her voice at seeing me, and it continued as she talked about her life and how I reminded her of her younger self. At this point, it became evident to me that healthcare isn't only about pills and needles but being able to sit and have a healthy conversation with a patient, showing compassion and being a beacon of hope.

That was the nursing dream I had always envisioned – a setting where patient care far exceeds pushing pills.

My journey has taught me patience, perseverance and the value of spending time with loved ones. I have learned to appreciate the simple things in life, such as a clean bill of health, being able to walk in the park, or simply have company. This is what most residents in a nursing home yearn for, and these are the very things we take for granted.

18

Winners Never Quit!

It amazes me that I have been practising as a nurse for 21 years. Interestingly, growing up, nursing was never an interest for me. I had grand ideas of becoming a chemical engineer, but that notion was quickly eroded with an interest in journalism. On reflection, I think I was fascinated with reporting and the limelight I thought it would bring.

It seems like it was just yesterday that I came to the end of my secondary school education tenure. I felt the great pressure of making my first life-changing decision: choosing a career. However, the socioeconomic status of my parents dictated my career path, and the choices were somewhat limited. Growing up in a very poor household meant that my dream of journalism had to be shelved. The choices were between pursuing a career in teaching or nursing, for neither of these required large tuition fees (at the time).

I was very fortunate to receive invitations to pursue studies in both professions, so I had to decide which one to accept. Teaching required payment of a small tuition fee; consequently, that career was also shelved. Nursing, then, was the forerunner of them all, for there were no fees, plus students were given a monthly allowance. These were the extra perks that aided my decision to pursue a career in nursing. I was delighted and well assured that there would be no added financial pressure on my parents.

The thought of leaving home to live without parental guidance or intrusion was exhilarating. I vividly remember counting down the months, weeks and days, down to the hours, minutes and seconds of the day, to be transported from my little semi-rural town to the huge metropolitan capital of Kingston, Jamaica. It was a bright Sunday afternoon, and the sun stood at attention with its rays in full beaming display when my mum and I boarded public transport with my solidly-packed bags. Mum had always been an integral source of support to me, so I was glad that she took this journey with me. Full of excitement and anticipation, we headed to my place of residence, which was within reasonably close proximity to the community college.

The defining moment eventually came: my first day at nursing school. Despite my eagerness, I felt very nervous and shy. I felt as though I was the smallest fish in the pond. It didn't take long, though, for me to make friendships, ones that have withstood the test of time.

The three years of training were intense, and there were days when I felt like quitting. But I was quick to remind myself that 'winners never quit' and 'quitters never win'. This became my anthem throughout my student days. I was driven and determined to endure to the end. Nurse training encompassed class-taught sessions as well as time in a hospital to gain practical experience.

Today, reminiscing on those years pursuing my career has highlighted the great moments I had in classes and on the wards.

Time went in a flash. In 1998, I graduated and joined the working class as a registered nurse. I was assigned to one of the prominent hospitals in Jamaica. Working in a hospital that served a very large geographical area with little resources was challenging. Overcrowded and understaffed wards became part of my normal routine, and the lack of major resources was a regular phenomenon. Concerns grew over my wellbeing, as I began to melt away in the eyes of my mother; my body weight was declining rapidly.

A typical workday started at 7:30am. Shifts were meant to finish at 3:30pm, but most days, I worked until 10:00pm. Every day, I was on my feet continuously, wading through the sea of patient beds on the ward. The needs of the patients were enormous, and the insufficient resources to meet their needs and expectations only exacerbated the situation. Mostly, lunch breaks were a very few minutes long, then I was rushing back to bedsides. Coupled with these challenges, there was little opportunity for career development for an ambitious newly qualified nurse.

It wasn't long before my zeal and enthusiasm for nursing began to diminish. My stomach turned just by the very thought of having to go to work. "There's got to be a better place to practice nursing and develop my full potential as a young nurse," I thought. It was evident that other nurses felt the same way. My level of despondency grew as time went on. It was most disheartening to realise that the challenges of the health system were not on the government's agenda and that no positive change was in sight. Within eighteen months, I needed an escape route.

I heard about other nurses who had successfully emigrated and were making very good use of their opportunities. Determined to do the same, I made enquiries and started emigration proceedings. I was so eager to leave that I completed applications to practice nursing in the United States, Bermuda and the United Kingdom. It took time for my documents to be processed and for my registration to practice to be agreed. I accepted the UK's offer as my nursing registration with the UKCC (which was later taken over by the NMC – the Nursing and Midwifery Council) was the first to be agreed. I then acquired a work permit to work at a nursing home in a very desirable area.

How excited I felt! It was a big dream come true. I was filled with delight, though saddened by the fact that I was leaving the hospital that had built my confidence and resilience as a registered nurse. I felt great regret about not staying to be part of the solution, for not being an agent to create an efficient and effective health system.

There were tears, hugs and long waves of goodbye as I boarded the flight to the UK. I was filled with a feeling of melancholy as I made myself comfortable in my seat. Later, I began to feel trepidation as my mind drifted to thoughts of the unknown that awaited me in the UK.

One early morning in August 2000, I disembarked the flight on my quest to practice nursing in a first world country that embodied a plethora of opportunities. I was promptly collected from the airport and taken to the nursing home. On arrival, the staff were very friendly, and I was greeted with English tea and biscuits. I was then whisked off to my accommodation with reassurances that I could stay for at least a month until I found a suitable place of my own.

It wasn't long before dismay arose. I was flabbergasted to be taken to an unoccupied resident's room! This was contrary to the contract I'd been given by the recruiting agency, which said appropriate accommodation would be provided. I did not consider this to be appropriate – it didn't even have a private shower facility! The first thought that came to me was to call a cab and head back to the airport. Later, I found out that the room had only become vacant the day before due to the death of a resident. I verbalised my disappointment to the manager who was present at my arrival, but she merely apologised and informed me that the recruiting agency was aware of the arrangements. I was very determined that I wasn't going to lay on that bed to rest, so I started the quest of finding a hotel for the night.

The following day, favour found me. One of the members of staff offered me a room in her home, and I was very grateful to stay with her for a few months until I found more suitable accommodation.

Though the nursing home itself was lovely, I did not enjoy working there. I yearned for the challenges and the development of skills that would enable me to attain my full potential. Unfortunately, the nursing home did not meet my expectations, so within six months, I broke the contract, paid the difference in full and moved on to work for the NHS.

I was so excited about the opportunity to work in a hospital setting in the UK. I worked on a surgical ward and was astonished by the wealth of resources at the doctor's and nurse's fingertips. I was surprised by the fact that patients were not required to pay for healthcare and by the prompt referrals they were given to have diagnostic investigations carried out. I was also surprised by the various mandatory training courses I had to attend, but I thoroughly enjoyed all areas of work. Initially, I found the team on the ward to be very supportive and encouraging.

After some time, the true culture of the surgical ward and the whole hospital became evident. Racism was well pronounced, for only colleagues of Caucasian origin were promoted and sent on courses for professional development. It was very demoralising. It was difficult to accept that my innovative and creative ideas for patient care were overlooked by my line manager and ward manager. However, I was determined to leap over any obstacles that tried to block or prevent my progress.

Despite working in that environment, the passion I had for nursing and delivering excellent care to patients was kept alive. Most patients were grateful for the care received, which was apparent from their feedback as well as the cards and chocolates they sent to the ward.

Soon, I developed an interest in intensive care nursing. A year later, I was successful at an interview and given a job to work in the intensive care unit (ICU), caring for very ill patients. It was very noticeable that the ICU staff were diverse in their various cultural backgrounds. However, yet again, only Caucasians were in leadership and management roles. I found this very interesting. Regardless of the engraved culture that existed, I was determined not to allow it to be a distraction or deterrent to my progress. I worked relentlessly hard, developed my assertiveness skills and pushed back on the doors that were shut in my face. I was not afraid to challenge those in leadership and management when inequality was evident. With my hard-working nature and high levels of motivation, I was able to keep focussed and pursue my goals of professional development.

My optimism, Christian virtues and positivity were the anchors that kept me going. The zeal I had for learning and academic development propelled me to acquire a diploma and a BSc degree in Intensive Care Nursing. All of which was fully funded by the hospital. I was so grateful!

My tenure in ICU lasted for eight years, in which time I got married and started a family. My priorities then changed, and I needed a job that did not require me to work night shifts, at weekends or on public holidays. My family are predominantly the essence of what I do; they are the motivation that pushes me to move forward. The quest of seeking a job that offered hours conducive to the care of young children led me to apply for a senior nurse practitioner post at the National Blood Service in a different part of the country. I have been working with the organisation for ten years now and have enjoyed every moment of it. I have been able to pursue a Master's degree with their support, which was incredible.

My training and work experience in Jamaica has remained well treasured, for they set the firm platform that allowed me to fulfil my dream and desire to develop skills and expertise. I have grown and developed in so many ways, both professionally and as a person, and I am very optimistic about what the future holds. Irrespective of all the peaks and valleys I've experienced here in the UK, I have no regrets about emigrating. Coming to the UK was a huge step, but I leapt on the steps of opportunities that arose, and I am very grateful to God for such a great blessing. I have evolved into a better person and have been able to be a support and tremendous blessing to family and friends back in Jamaica.

On reflection, I am happy that I was bold enough to take that huge step of faith in quest of reaching my full potential as a nurse. My advice to others contemplating emigration would be: Think about what you want to achieve, think about your current situation and evaluate the possible gains that exist against the possible losses. If you are a believer, pray and seek direction from your God, then allow Him to lead and direct your path.

19

Nursing in the UK

Immigration officer: How long do you intend to stay in the UK?

Me: I'm here for three weeks (I replied as I had been advised to and as I had rehearsed back home before my adventure into the unknown).

Immigration officer: What do you do in Zimbabwe?

Me: I am a nurse.

Immigration officer: What does your husband do?

Me: He is a telecoms technician.

Immigration officer: Do you have children?

Me: Yes, I have three children.

Immigration officer: What are their ages?

Me: 5, 4 and 1.

Immigration officer: They are quite young. Who is looking after them while you are here?

Me: My husband.

Immigration officer: Why didn't you bring the youngest child?

Me: My husband wanted me to have a break on my own. That's why I came alone.

Immigration officer: How much do you have to spend during your stay?

Me: £200.

Immigration officer: That's too little for accommodation and food.

Me: Well, my host has promised to provide my food and accommodation.

Immigration officer: So, how much did you pay for your ticket?

Me: £400.

Immigration officer: Ok, wait here for a few minutes. I will be with you shortly.

The officer went into another office with my passport and came back a few minutes later, as promised.

Immigration officer: We just want to find out a bit more about your visit, so please come with me.

I was taken to an office where I was interrogated for about 9 hours. All I knew was that we had purchased my ticket from a travel agent in Zimbabwe for £400. What I didn't know, but soon found out from the immigration officer, was that it was a free ticket that was not supposed to have been sold. Thus, the immigration office wanted proof that I had purchased the ticket. He wanted to satisfy himself that I had not come to work illegally. It was gruelling, but I was later released to meet up with a friend who had come to pick me up from the airport. It was May 1992. The rest is history.

I had completed my general nursing training in Harare from 1983-1986. I got married the same year I graduated, then moved to join my husband in another part of Zimbabwe, where I worked at two different hospitals successively. Towards the end of 1991, I stumbled across some information about nursing in the UK.

I made some enquiries about registering with the then UKCC (United Kingdom Central Council for Nursing, Midwifery and Health Visiting) to practice as a qualified nurse in the UK. I submitted an application and was requested to complete an overseas nurses programme to prepare me for working as a nurse in the UK. It was difficult to secure a place for this course while in Zimbabwe, so I came as a visitor to the UK on a 6-month visitor visa to seek a place on this much-cherished course.

After a few weeks, I was offered a place on the course at a general hospital, but it didn't start until September. Once the studies started, I was able to extend my visa to see me through the duration of the 3-month course. The programme itself was fairly straightforward as Zimbabwean nursing training is founded on British standards. The language was easy, too, as I had learned English throughout my schooling.

While studying, I managed to get part-time work with a nurse who was providing 24-hour care for a ventilated Middle Eastern client in a nearby hospital. I did not have much experience with ventilators, but this nurse was kind enough to teach me all I needed to know. This job paid ten times more than what I had been earning in Zimbabwe, so it was a real boost to our finances.

In December 1992, I successfully completed the overseas nursing programme, and the following month, I registered with the UKCC. I then started working for a nursing agency, earning a fairly decent amount per hour. One thing I had not realised was the differences between the role of a nurse in Zimbabwe and England. I found that there were limits to what I could do, even things that I considered to be part of a nurse's role (based on my Zimbabwean background). One example: When one of my patients needed a cannula, I just looked for one and was about to insert it when someone asked, "Have you been assessed to do that?" My answer was that I had always done it back home. Of course, I was stopped, for I had not been assessed locally for this extended role. I was shocked to learn that inserting cannulas was not part of the English basic nurse training. I had been taught how to do so very early in my training in Zimbabwe. I was very frustrated by these simple limitations in my practice as a nurse.

My husband managed to join me in the UK in October 1992 to study engineering, but my pride and joy (my children) were still back home in Zimbabwe. I cried a lot, and we were both uncertain about whether our children would be able to join us. What we lacked was sound advice regarding settling in the UK. We lacked information. The only information we received was negative; we were told about how difficult it is to settle as immigrants in the UK, and we were told to dodge the police.

Little did I know that this information was not relevant to me, as I had a qualification that enabled me to get a work permit. So, when my visitor's visa expired, I struggled unnecessarily with my immigration status when I could have just taken a permanent job where my employer would have applied for a work permit on my behalf (agencies do not apply for work permits).

Early in 1993, I discovered that I was pregnant. Due to problems with all of my previous pregnancies, I could not work, so I stayed at home for the duration of the pregnancy and relied on handouts from well-wishers. In the meantime, my husband had his visa renewed to student status, and I became his dependent. Eventually, I got my National Insurance number. During this period, we also managed to obtain a council flat and set up Child Benefit for the new baby. Finally, to our delight, just before child number four arrived, our other three children joined us in the UK.

Just two weeks after giving birth, I called the agency to tell them I was ready for work. I had little choice, for I was not entitled to any other social support, so I had to sweat it out two weeks postpartum and leave my newborn with my husband.

As my confidence increased in working in the UK, I applied for a job at a top children's hospital, and I was successful. The experience I gained working there was priceless. I worked as a bank nurse, which meant I could choose my shifts and share childcare responsibilities with my student husband.

Three years later, I became tired of doing agency and bank work, so I looked for a permanent post and secured a position in a recovery ward at another hospital. Out of all the places I have worked in the UK, this was the best, and it's somewhere to which I would willingly return. The manager was a white South African lady, the best manager I have ever had in my working life. She pushed us all to develop ourselves professionally by sending us on courses and initiating promotions. She was even concerned about our personal wellbeing. She united the team so well that we felt like a family. I will never forget her kindness. She caused me to love working in recovery.

Sadly, I had to leave that job because my husband was offered employment in another part of the country. When we made the move in 1999, I got a job on the recovery ward of a local hospital. I honestly endured working there, because the standards were much lower than where I had come from. However, I stayed with that ward until 2002 when I left for an ICU job at the same hospital. I am grateful for all the experience I gained at that hospital, but I felt a glass ceiling prevented me from going for higher managerial posts. So, I left to work full-time with an agency.

While working my notice, the manager warned me that it was not nice for agency nurses and said that I could return to the hospital if things became too hard for me. But it is now sixteen years since I left, and I have not regretted it at all! I enjoy the freedom of working as and when I want; I don't need to negotiate for any holidays or days off, and I feel like I am in control of my working life. I've even furthered my studies – self-funded – by completing a Master's degree in public health. I am hoping, one day, to put this qualification into practice.

Working as a full-time agency nurse has been another experience to cherish. I have worked in hospitals and in the community. It has been amazing how differently people have received me in their environments. As a black nurse in a white-dominated environment, at times, I was made to feel out of place, especially when I went into people's homes. I used to worry about facing racism, but over the years, I have developed a thick skin. Even though I am still sometimes hurt by people's comments, I always make my feelings known to the agency. I have learned that, in life, one cannot be loved by everyone nor hated by everybody. So, as an agency worker, if I'm not welcome in one place, I go to the next one. Life goes on.

Now, it is 28 years since I first stepped into the UK as a visitor. I believe I have gained good experience from working here as a nurse, experience that I can transfer to anywhere in the world.

Nursing in the UK has had its ups and downs, but I would not exchange it for anything. When I was nursing in Zimbabwe, we had a shortage of everything except patients. It was a frustrating time in my career, and I had desperately looked for a way out of that environment. I love caring for sick people, but without resources, it's like trying to empty a swimming pool with a teaspoon. In comparison, nursing in the UK has been a joyful time in my career, as it has given me the satisfaction of providing the best care I can for sick people. Though, saying that, I wish I could do the same among the underprivileged back home.

The only downside of nursing in the UK has been the lack of opportunities to progress, and I noticed that the chances increased or decreased based upon where I lived. Now, though, things seem to be changing for foreign nurses, and more opportunities are arising.

So, my advice to younger nurses of colour is to embrace every opportunity to progress in your career. Make yourself marketable, go into specialised areas, and gain a lot of experience and knowledge, giving yourself the chance of working anywhere.

So far, I am satisfied with my career, and I have no regrets of having branched into nursing from school.

20

Your Face Fits

———————

y journey to a career in nursing in diaspora was one of chance. With a background in statistics and computer science, I came to the UK in 2002 intending to do a Master's degree in statistics. However, before that even became a possibility, an opportunity came my way, via a third party, to be a project worker in a drug and alcohol unit. I had not met a drug user before in my life but decided to give it a go.

Following a very rigorous interview process, I got the job! I found that nearly one-fourth of the service users were BAME (Black, Asian or Minority Ethnic). Despite this, there was hardly any BAME staff; I was one of very few.

Before this opportunity came, I had worked in various care assistant roles, both within nursing homes and homes for people with learning disabilities. I did not enjoy the former at all, as I found the jobs too physically strenuous, but I did enjoy the latter, especially working with people with mild cases of Down's syndrome.

The opportunity to work within the drug and alcohol team was, therefore, quite refreshing. I truly enjoyed this unlikely role. After nearly two years, my mentor and supervisor advised me to do a degree in mental health nursing so that I could have a proper career in this field. I took her advice and completed my training in 2010.

My first job as a qualified nurse was on the assessment ward of a medium-secure mental health unit with forensic patients (people who had committed serious crimes but judged by a court as having 'diminished responsibility' due to a mental health issue). It came as quite a big shock, particularly because some of the patients were very violent. As a student nurse, I had not been exposed to such a setting, neither had I worked with patients who were so acutely unwell. Nevertheless, I did enjoy some aspects of my role.

As a member of staff, I soon realised that a person's face either fitted or it didn't. For example, it often happened that a BAME applicant would be interviewed for a job opening, then we would later be told that "so and so" did not get the job because their face did not fit, they were not friendly enough, or they appeared lazy. I was quite intrigued by these descriptions of fellow BAME individuals, so I subconsciously became a person whose face *did* fit – I smiled a lot, offered to make cups of tea, and generally worked really hard.

The black staff experienced a lot of discrimination, both from the patients and managers. We were the ones exposed to the most dangerous patients, and we were the ones required to work in the most difficult wards.

It is also noteworthy that a good number of our patients were white people. Unofficially, we were informed that when a white person committed a crime, they were more likely to end up in hospital as a mental health patient than in prison as a criminal. Some of these white patients were genuinely unwell at the time of the crime, but others just knew how to play the system.

Conversely, people of colour were more likely to be criminalised and remain behind bars.

I had been working in this secure environment for almost a year when I was involved in an awful experience that resulted in me suffering an industrial injury. This necessitated being signed off work for six months.

When it came time for me to return to work, my confidence was very low, but I did not give up. Rather, I chose to step down to a rehabilitation ward within the same medium-secure unit. I must admit, though, that the support for nurses was very poor. We had huge responsibilities, but we were over-worked and under-paid, and all of our benefits had been stripped away. It reached the point of just not being worth my while remaining in that kind of environment.

Therefore, a year later, I left that unit to move into community care, working with people who were still considered acutely mentally ill but didn't need to be in a hospital. My role involved providing treatment to patients in their own homes. This was a much better experience, although I still lacked the much-needed support since there was not enough clinical supervision.

Our client group was very risky, however, and we did lose quite a few young people within a short space of time, mostly to suicide. This concerned me a great deal, and I realised that my nursing degree didn't include the training needed to manage this client group. Additionally, there was not enough recognition of the impact of mental health issues, particularly on young people.

Overall, the work was very interesting, and I did meet some very awesome clients and staff. One such colleague was a gentleman from Zimbabwe who introduced me to the world of interim working (it's similar to working freelance, but interim work tends to be more specific and temporary). This gentleman showed my husband (who is also a mental health nurse) and me how to set up a limited company from which we hired ourselves out as interim workers. This opened up possibilities we had never imagined, and it became our way of life. Interim working is not for everyone, but my husband and I have benefitted immensely from it, and we have never looked back. There are associated risks, but these can be overcome.

About six months into our new way of working, I realised I was never meant to be a nurse but one of the brains behind change. My dream was to be a consultant to the NHS in terms of managing change and bringing a much-needed breath of fresh air to the system. But this was not an easy opening to get, especially because of the discrimination against minority groups. It would be another two years before my dream became a reality.

During those two years, I continued to work as an interim, but I also undertook lots of research into how I could support the NHS with some of the problems I could see. I studied PRINCE2, a project management course, which opened my eyes to so many things.

The time finally came when I secured a job as an advisor to the NHS clinical commissioning groups (CCGs), working in what is termed as 'continuing healthcare'. My advisory role has generally meant being involved in drafting policies and processes as well as supporting the CCGs and their partner agencies to restructure and work more productively. It's a role I truly enjoy, and I have definitely found my niche in life. I have increased my knowledge through continued learning, and I have gained so much vital managerial expertise in this minefield of work. It has also exposed me to higher levels of management and given me an understanding of how the NHS functions and how the different systems integrate within England and the UK as a whole. I have worked at a fairly senior level, supporting commissioning agendas, and I have been very instrumental in developing and implementing work streams that support patient flow.

But sadly, there are few BAME people in senior management. They have been relegated to menial tasks, however bright and intelligent they are. I have worked within five CCGs so far, and not one has a BAME person at the very top. I do wonder if it is because we do not apply for those roles or because we do not get selected for interviews. Since working at a more senior level, I have sat on interview panels and have seen for myself that institutional racism that comes to the surface; thankfully, I have been able to speak out against it and get justice for the right candidate despite their background.

Although nursing as a career was not on my radar when I left my country, it has been the pathway that led me to where I am today, for which I am grateful. The different elements of my job are so fulfilling, and when I consider that I have no background in law, I realise just how adaptable humans are, and how we can be so useful given the right opportunities. I do believe that what I have learned and experienced will be applied somewhere else in life, wherever that may be. I am tempted to establish a specific care pathway for elderly BAME people, but I'm not entirely sure this is what I want to be doing post-retirement!

In my opinion, the NHS is one of the best health organisations in the world, so despite all its problems, it does need to be upheld. Currently, my husband and I are working on an exciting project with our local MP, documenting and evidencing some of the failings within CCGs and offering solutions to make our valuable NHS function better.

On a more personal note, my desire for all BAME nurses is to strive for excellence in their current roles and to become aware of the opportunities for progression. Our expertise as clinicians is very valuable and, although not appreciated all of the time, remains absolutely vital.

To conclude, my advice to people desiring to join the nursing sector is that it can open many doors. At the same time, though, it can limit your potential if you conform to the norms of life. It appears there is only so much one can do and achieve as a nurse in the UK. If you possess a passion for nursing, then, by all means, get started in a nursing career. If you are already a nurse, please think outside the box and educate yourself to keep relevant.

Conclusion

Thank you for joining our nurses as they have shared honestly about their experiences of living and working in diaspora. Though nursing in a foreign land did not come easy for most, they persevered, demonstrating their passion for this vital profession.

In the introduction of this book, we highlighted racism as one of the major challenges that confronted our contributors. You've now read how that played out in terms of verbal abuse and barriers in career progression. The former seems to go unreported, while the latter supports other findings in the UK, such as the *Workforce Race Equality Standard* published by NHS England in 2019[3]. Although steps have been made to improve the career prospects of BAME staff, their data confirmed that *"their access to opportunities for development and progression still do not yet correspond with those of their white colleagues; the gap is still stark in many places."* In addition, *The Guardian* newspaper has

---

3 https://improvement.nhs.uk/documents/6181/wres-nursing-strategy.pdf

reported on the systematic racism as well as the ethnic pay-gap that exists within the NHS[4].

This data, combined with the accounts we have presented, shows that there is still a long road to travel to achieve equality. However, we acknowledge and are grateful that NHS England is taking measures to remove systematic discrimination and inequality. We hope it will be the beginning of greater changes nationwide.

* * *

To our fellow immigrant nurses:

Let nothing stop you from achieving your dreams. As difficult as it may be, don't give up. Nursing is hard work, and it requires passion, care and dedication. Your contribution to humanity does not go unnoticed by everyone. Remain resilient despite the challenges that come your way. You can achieve the success you are striving for, and we trust that these stories will inspire you to keep going.

---

4 https://www.theguardian.com/society/2020/jun/09/nhs-blood-unit-systematically-racist-internal-report-finds; https://www.theguardian.com/commentisfree/2018/oct/01/black-nurse-nhs-doctors-nurses-prejudices

Our greatest ability as humans is not to change the world, but to change ourselves.

MAHATMA GANDHI

Share with Us!

We hope you have been challenged and inspired by the stories in this book. Whether or not you can identify with our contributors, we hope you have been able to empathise with immigrant nurses living and working in diaspora and that you have enjoyed reading this book as much as we have enjoyed compiling and writing it. We would love to hear your thoughts, reactions or comments to any of the stories. Please get in touch: admin@talesindiaspora.com

* * *

For more information about this book and others in the diaspora series, join our mailing list, follow us on social media or visit our website: **www.talesindiaspora.com**

About the Authors

Audry Sibindi and Grace Maworera are both healthcare professionals who have lived in diaspora for the past 18 years. Their own experiences and challenges of being immigrant nurses sparked their passion for sharing the stories of others in the same position. Fundamentally, the message they desire to communicate is that healthcare professionals living in diaspora are not alone – if they feel unsafe, at-risk or experience inequality at work, they should speak up.

Audry and Grace currently live with their families in England and Ireland, respectively.